D1062958

Man,
Master
of His Destiny

Translated from the French
Original title : L'HOMME A LA CONQUÊTE
DE SA DESTINÉE

Omraam Mikhaël Aïvanhov

Man,
Master
of His Destiny

4th edition

Izvor Collection — No. 202

PROSVETA

Prosveta S.A – B.P.12 – 83601 Fréjus CEDEX (France)

ISSN 0763-2738
ISBN 2-85566-377-6
originale edition: ISBN 2-85566-344-X

TABLE OF CONTENTS

1

THE LAW OF CAUSE AND EFFECT

I

Man cannot perform even the slightest act without inevitably triggering certain forces which, just as inevitably, produce certain effects. This notion of the relation of cause to effect was primordial in the original meaning of the word *karma*. It was only later that Karma was taken to mean the debt incurred by past misdeeds.

Karma-yoga, one of the many different yogas which exist in India, is nothing more than a discipline which teaches individuals to develop themselves through disinterested activities destined to set them free. It is when man acts with covetousness, cunning and dishonesty that he begins to incur debts and it is then that Karma takes on the meaning which is now commonly attributed to it: punishment for faults committed in the past.

In point of fact it would be true to say that Karma – in the second sense of the word – becomes operative whenever anyone does something which is less than perfect and, of course, this includes almost every one of our actions! But man proceeds by trial and error. He needs to practise before he can do something perfectly and as long as he goes on making mistakes, he has to correct and make up for them and this entails hard work and suffering.

You will perhaps be tempted to conclude that since we inevitably make mistakes in all our actions and that this entails suffering and reparation, it would be far better to do nothing! Not at all. One must act. It is true, of course, that you will suffer, but you will learn, you will evolve, and then one day you will suffer no more. Once you have learned to work correctly there will be no more Karma for you. It is a fact that every gesture, every word, triggers certain forces which lead to certain consequences. But if your words and gestures were inspired by lovingkindness, purity and altruism, they would trigger beneficial effects. This is known as *dharma*.

Dharma is the result of well-ordered, harmonious, beneficial actions. Someone who is capable of acting in that way frees himself from the dominion of fate and falls under the law of Providence. It is no good trying to avoid trouble and suffering by avoiding all action; the best way is to be active, dynamic and full of initiative but, instead of acting from egoism and self-interest, to act only from higher motives. This is the only way to avoid disastrous consequences. It is utterly impossible to escape consequences: one way or another there are bound to be causes and consequences whatever you do. The thing to remember is that if you manage to act unselfishly, then the consequences will not be painful but joyful and happy and liberating.

If you choose to do nothing in the hope of being left in peace, you will never grow, you will never learn, you will never earn any reward; you will make no mistakes, but you will be a stone. Stones don't make mistakes! It is far better to make mistakes and even to get a bit dirty, but to learn something. If you have a building full of workmen how can you expect not to find plaster or smears of paint on the floor? It is asking the impossible. The smears have to be expected and they don't matter as long as the work gets done and the building goes up. Once the house is finished and all the dirty work done, then you can scrub and polish, and change into your tidy clothes. But at least the job is done.

One day, the Master Peter Deunov said, 'I give each one of you a little book from which to learn your alphabet (in Bulgarian we say: *boukvartché*. Perhaps you would say a First Reader). A year later, when I ask you for it, some of you give it back in perfect condition, absolutely clean and new. Having never opened it, they have learned nothing. Others on the contrary, give it back to me stained, marked and dog-eared. They have opened and closed it hundreds of times, they have carried it with them every-where, they have eaten over its open pages. Yes, but now they can read!' And the Master con-cluded, 'I prefer the second category.' I remem-ber I was very young at the time and I shyly asked him which category I was in. 'You?' he said, 'you're in the second category.' I was de-lighted because I had understood that it was bet-ter.

Well, I don't know what condition the *bouk-vartché* was in when I gave it back to him, but in any event he put me into the category of those who want to get the job done, and he was right! It does not matter how many mistakes you make, how many stains you get on your book or how much paint you splash about. It doesn't matter if people criticize you or swear at you, all that is of no importance. What does matter is that you learn to read, to get the job done, to fin-ish building your house. People who are always cautious and afraid to commit themselves never make any progress. Where will all that caution get them?

In the Apocalypse it is written that we must be either hot or cold, not lukewarm, for the Lord 'spews out the lukewarm'. How is it that some people seem to prefer to be lukewarm? The world has no use for such people. Don't be afraid to make mistakes! If you want to learn a foreign language and are so frightened of making a mistake that you never open your mouth, you will never learn! And it is just the same with Karma: you must not be paralysed by the fear of making mistakes which you will have to pay for. Gradually, as you practise and learn to act from a divine motive, you will attract not the negative effects of Karma, but the positive effects of Dharma: an abundance of grace and blessings.

II

No one can evade the law of cause and effect. It is utterly impossible. What is possible, and extremely important, is to know what kind of forces one is unleashing by one's acts. And this is why I say that the most marvellous law given to us by Cosmic Intelligence can be found where no one ever thinks of looking for it, where scholars, theologians and philosophers never look any more: in nature, and in particular in agriculture. Yes, I mean it: agriculture. Every farmer knows that if you plant a fig-tree you will not get grapes from it, and that an apple tree will produce apples, not pears. And there you have it, the greatest of all moral laws: 'As you sow so shall you reap.'

Farmers were mankind's first moral philosophers, it was they who first understood that the intelligence of nature had decreed this stern and immutable law: the law of cause and effect.

Later, when they saw how human beings lived, they found that the same law applied : if you behave with cruelty, selfishness and violence, sooner or later you will be a victim of your own cruelty, selfishness and violence. This law is also known as the law of echo reflection, or the boomerang effect. The ball you hit bounces back and hits you.

'As you sow so shall you reap.' If you study this basic law closely you will see how far-reaching it is. It becomes a deeply meaningful system, for all the essential truths can be applied in all areas of life. A detailed understanding of this law can engender a whole philosophy and that is why there are now so many rules and regulations in religion. At the origin of all these rules is one law : you can reap only what you have sown. Other laws equally true have been added to this one, extending and enlarging it into a full-fledged philosophy, and Jesus' words, 'Do not unto others what you would not have them do to you,' are simply an application of this one law.

Those who try to deny or reject these basic laws become more and more estranged from Truth : their souls are torn by doubt and anxiety, they are forever tossed about on the storms of life. And yet the truth is very simple, it is staring them in the face. Why do modern thinkers refuse to see it and persist in offering their own theories, invented in utter disregard of Cosmic Intelligence? As they no longer believe in a moral law based on the laws of nature their reasoning is false and the conclusions they reach are false. Those who read their books and are gullible enough to accept their teaching fall into the same error and end up in terrible anguish and darkness. So, take care! You have to learn to reason and make judgments. If you have no criteria to guide you, you can be led into error by the first person who comes along. Be on your guard and don't let yourself be influenced by clouded human intellects. Follow the guidance of the Intelligence which has so marvellously ordered and arranged everything.

Even if you do not believe in God you cannot fail to recognize that there is an order in nature and, consequently, that there must be an Intelligence which created that order. Reflect for a moment on the fact that each seed reproduces its own kind. How is it possible not to see that this must be the work of a higher Intelligence? The mere recognition of this law is enough to make us change our vision of the world. You may not believe in God, but you cannot deny the fact that every seed produces its own kind exactly, whether it be a plant, a tree, an insect, an animal or a man. This law is absolute and it should cause you to reflect. Perhaps you think you are entitled to be ungrateful, unjust, cruel or violent, but you must know that sooner or later this law will catch up with you and you will see its application in your own life. If you have children, for instance, they will resemble you and through them you will suffer from the very things that you yourself have done. Even if God does not exist, you have endless proof of the fact that a Cosmic Intelligence exists.

You persist in doing whatever you like, convinced that you will never have to suffer the consequences: well, believe what you like, nothing will alter the fact that Cosmic Intelligence has already recorded everything you do. You have put a seed, a germ, into every single thought, feeling or act, and that seed grows: if you have been ungrateful, unjust, cruel and violent, one fine day you will come up against the same ingratitude, the same injustice, the same cruelty and the same violence. They will bounce back and strike you, twenty, thirty or forty years later, and when this happens, you will begin to understand that Cosmic Intelligence does, indeed, exist and that everything is recorded. If you want to have nothing to do with the Bible and the Gospels, the Prophets, the churches and the temples, you are perfectly free to ignore them, but you must, at least, give credence to this absolutely irrefutable law: 'As you sow so shall you reap.' 'Sow the wind and reap the whirlwind', said the sages of old who knew how things worked. As for the scholars and thinkers of today who reject this truth, well, they too will find themselves cornered and stricken one day. It is inevitable. They cannot escape the consequences of their acts and, perhaps, when this law begins to catch up with them, they will understand. If they are so intelligent, how is it they cannot see something so simple and obvious? I will go so far as to say that if you take this law as your starting point, it is possible to reconstruct all the sacred books the world has ever known, just from this one law.

A lot of people say, 'It's all very well, the Bible, the Gospels, say thus and so, but we don't even know for sure that God exists.' I would like to tell these people that they need not bother their heads about the existence of God; they don't need to know if Jesus really lived nor if the Gospels are authentic, all they need to do is recognize this one law. It is enough to make everything fall into place: it leads to the Truth. You see, my explanation is very simple. Even if God did not exist, this law would make it necessary to invent Him! So why let yourselves be hoodwinked by so-called fashionable thinkers whose one idea is to undermine everything? Instead of helping human beings to recognize the simple truths which are visible to the naked eye, they are forever leading them astray with their 'original' ideas. Even if their theories are utterly in contradiction with the truth that is written into the whole of nature, that makes no difference: as long as they are new and original everyone is bewitched!

Moral law is a reality, but human beings are blind and fail to see it and continue to argue about God or points of theology. It is pointless to argue. The only thing that matters is to know that everything is recorded. Absolutely everything. If Nature has so ordained things that a tree records in its seed all its properties, its colour and dimensions and the taste and perfume of its fruit, why should it not be the same for man? Nature has succeeded in recording everything, and the moral law is based on this: Nature's memory. You may be astonished, but yes, Nature does have a memory and nothing can ever erase what it has once recorded. It will be just too bad for the person who decides to discount this memory! Day and night, it records the cacophony, the disorder that reigns within him and one day he will be crushed, struck down, wiped out. No one can escape this law. No one

has ever had the power to escape it, be he emperor or dictator. No one! In Nature's memory
everything is on record. So, be careful. Whatever
you do, think or wish, is recorded in the depths
of your own cells and one day, sooner or later,
you will reap the harvest in your own life. You
can create another, happier destiny for yourself
only if you take care not to sow the seeds of
darkness and destruction through your words,
thoughts and acts.

You must not believe that those who are
kind and generous and full of love, get only
knocks in return. People who are in too much of
a hurry to draw their conclusions spread this
stupid idea that if you are too kind it will only
bring you suffering. This is simply not true.
Good always produces good and evil always produces evil. If you do good you will receive it in
return, whether you want to or not. If you do
good and receive evil in return it is because there
are still people on this earth who abuse your
kindness and try to profit from it; if you are patient and persevere, sooner or later they will be
punished, eliminated by someone else who is
stronger and still more violent, and then they
will understand and repent and come to you to
atone for all the wrong they did you. So good always bears fruit; in fact, it bears fruit twofold,
because in cases like this, Heaven counts in your

favour all that you suffered by doing what was right, all the undeserved misfortunes that befell you, and your reward will be double.

Today, men stand in dire need of complete, truthful and incontestable knowledge and it is this knowledge that I bring you. Go ahead, try to deny that you reap whatever you have sown! Of course, everyone is convinced on all that concerns the physical plane, but that is not enough. If they looked a little further and a little higher they would find the same law at work on all levels. For the world is one, and on every level and at every stage the same phenomena can be found, although always in different, more subtle forms.

Whatever you find on earth can be found also in water. And whatever is in water exists in air, and so on. All four elements obey the same laws, but as their essence and their density are not the same you will find some differences in the way they apply those laws. They react more or less rapidly, more or less violently, but they are governed by identical principles. Man's mind, for instance, is analogous to air: the eddies and currents of the mind are the same as those of the atmosphere, only in the subtler form of ideas and thoughts. The laws governing the psychic plane are identical with those which govern physical nature.

When a gardener fails to find something in his garden which he did not plant, instead of being furious or revolted, he thinks, 'Well, old man, you never had time to sow any carrot seed, so you won't have any carrots this year. Never mind, you will have plenty of lettuce and onions and parsley, because you sowed them.' Human beings seem to be very knowledgeable about agriculture; when it comes to fruit or vegetables they know exactly how things work, but as soon as they get into the area of the soul or the mind all their learning vanishes and they think they can reap happiness, joy and peace although they have sown nothing but violence, cruelty and malice. Don't you believe it! All they will reap is the same violence, cruelty and malice and if they storm and rage all it proves is that they are not good farmers!

The very first rule of moral law is never to allow yourself a thought, a feeling or an action that could be harmful or dangerous to someone else, because you will be obliged, one day, to eat the fruit of those seeds you have sown, and if they were poisonous it is you who will be poisoned! The day you begin to take this as an absolute rule you will be on the path to perfection. Of course, I know that what misleads people is the fact that these laws take so long to show their effects: neither reward nor punishment comes at once. One man may break all the laws and yet be highly successful in everything he undertakes, whereas another who is perfectly honest and always doing good, has endless difficulties: so everyone draws the conclusion that there is no justice. Human beings do not know why reward and punishment are so long in coming. If they ever think about it, they wonder if it would not be much better if the effects of the laws made themselves felt at once so that they would understand at once.

Let me tell you why the effects of our acts are so long in coming. As you will see, it is just one more proof of the lovingkindness and mercy of Cosmic Intelligence. It is to give men time to learn from experience, to reflect, to repent and even improve, thereby wiping out past mistakes. If punishment was meted out at once we would be annihilated and would never have a chance to improve. Heaven gives us the time we need, sending us a few little problems along the way to encourage us to think and to give us a chance to make reparation.

But those who do only what is right do not receive their reward immediately, either. And it is better that they should not, because if they were rewarded at once they too might slacken their efforts and begin to break all the laws. Heaven leaves them time to become stronger, to

consolidate their gains and to get to know themselves better. If they are not rewarded immediately it is so that they may be tested and show
how persevering they will be in doing right. So,
you see, there are good reasons for the delays.
But, make no mistake about it, good always produces good fruit, this is an absolute truth. And
evil always ends badly, and this is also absolute!
The only question is how long it takes for a
cause to produce its effects.

Obviously, when the world is falling apart all
around one it takes great firmness and determi-
nation, great willpower and strength and indo-
mitable faith to persevere in doing right. But it is
precisely in these conditions that there is great
merit in doing so. When conditions are ideal,
when everything runs smoothly, when everything is pleasant and favourable, it is all too easy
to believe in good and behave accordingly. No,
no! It is now, when things are going from bad to
worse that it is meritorious to persevere in doing
what is right without being swayed or under-
mined by bad conditions. A disciple, a Master,
always tries to count only on the strength of his
own spirit. In the midst of the very worst conditions he will summon to his aid his inner resources of goodwill, love and light. This is the
mark of the truly spiritual man. If one relied on
their words, a great many people would seem to

be deeply spiritual, but when one sees that they are bowled over by the slightest adversity one is forced to ask, 'Where is the power of the spirit they're always boasting about?'

Everybody expects others to be thoughtful, kind, patient and indulgent with them. That's all very well, but how do you obtain this happy state of affairs? By being, oneself, thoughtful, kind, patient and indulgent with others. If you want people to behave well towards you, you have to behave well towards them first. You will surely say, 'Oh, we know all that.' Yes, you know all that, but only in theory. There are still millions of people in the world who are rude, hard-hearted and cruel, and who are surprised and hurt when others behave in the same way to them. They are convinced that it is the others who should submit and comply with their wishes. But just observe their behaviour: they expect to get satisfactory results although the means they use are in direct contradiction to the results they hope for, and they refuse to believe that if they sowed seeds of gentleness, love and kindness, they too would be treated with gentleness love and kindness. I do assure you: even if someone behaves badly and is disagreeable and unkind to you, as long as you persevere in wishing him well and do nothing to harm him, he will end by laying down his arms.

If you want to receive affection and trust, you have to call for them. I can hear you say, 'I keep calling for them and they don't come!' No, when I say, 'Call for them', I mean you have to summon them from within yourself. You have to produce them. When you produce good things in yourself you can be one hundred percent sure you will find them in others too. It is when you produce them in yourself that you attract them to you. That is the magic of it. Why not give it a try? If you want to receive something which is very important to you, try first of all to give it to others. You cannot receive what you have not given. You may say, 'That's not true. Look at all the bigwigs who are rich and important and who give nothing, they're cold and contemptuous and yet they receive respect and esteem and honours from all sides.' That is simply because they have honoured others in a previous incarnation, so now it is their turn to receive honours. But if they continue to be haughty and unloving, they will end by receiving the same treatment from others later on.

The secret of success, the secret of true happiness, is to manifest in your own behaviour all that you would like to receive from others. If you want smiles and kind looks, offer smiles and kind looks to others. If you want an Angel, a Heavenly Being to come and instruct and guide you, find someone who has had less opportunity to learn, and start by sharing your light with him. Your actions will be reflected immediately in the Invisible World and spirits of light will be drawn to help you in the same way.

Yes, indeed! This is an extremely powerful law and it can be applied in many other areas. To smile and receive a smile in return is such a little thing: you gave a smile and it was returned! You have been kind and friendly to someone and he has been kind and friendly to you. Good! You have exchanged civilities and that is excellent, it is necessary, and it makes you feel good! But you must apply the same law in other areas to trigger results far more important than a smile, a handshake, a friendly glance, or some kind words in passing. You can set the whole universe in motion with this law, and this is where it becomes really interesting: to be able to reach out into faraway regions and influence even the most distant areas in space!

You can only reap fruits which correspond to the seeds you have sown. Now, of course, there may be all kinds of bad weather: the sun may have been too hot and burned all the crops, perhaps there was a drought, or birds and moles have eaten all your seeds. That is another question. Those are simply accidents which change nothing of the reality of the law. The innate properties of the seed cannot be taken away. It can be prevented from bringing forth fruit, but nothing can alter its nature. And that is what I am talking about: the nature of the seed.

So, if you are always very friendly and polite and all you get in return is four-letter words, no matter! That is a detail! Besides, you have to see who treats you like that and when and in what circumstances. Perhaps you have been too kind, too charitable and generous and too trusting and, if so, other people probably think you're an imbecile and you are a victim of the transitory conventions of mankind. But this is unimportant and, in any case, it won't last for ever, for people and circumstances are constantly changing, but the law does not change. When true values are restored, everything will fall into place once again and you will receive the good that you have sown.

In the world as it is today, you have to be tough to be appreciated. You have to ride rough-shod over others and be aggressive and thoroughly unpleasant. If you do this, people think you are somebody worthwhile! But that doesn't last forever either. Sooner or later another, an even tougher character will come along and then it will be your turn to be victimized. You must not let yourselves be influenced by a situation which is only temporary: if you are observant you will see that violent people always end by being ill-treated by others more violent than they.

So don't be in too much of a hurry to raise all kinds of objections. I know all the objections you could make far better than you, because I never wait for others to raise objections, I do so myself and then I seize my own arguments by the throat and worry the life out of them and, if they stand up to my attacks I know that they are gold, pure gold! And if they are gold then they are the truth. And what about an argument which fails to survive my rough treatment? Well, it only remains to bury it deep and dark: *Requiescat in pace.* Problem solved!

Now, let me paint a picture for you: imagine a vast and magnificent forest. Its trees are loaded with all kinds of beautiful flowers and succulent fruit; it is teeming with birds and animals and all kinds of good things. But there is just one snag: it is surrounded by a very high, very thick wall, which means no one can get in. There is even broken glass and barbed wire on the wall and as if that were not enough, the forest is full of dangerous animals: bears, lions, tigers who ask nothing better than to dine off the imprudent intruder. The problem is that you need some of that lovely fruit. How can you get at it? All of a

sudden you notice some monkeys in the trees
and you know you are saved. You take a bag of
oranges and you go close to the wall and start
pelting the monkeys with your oranges. In no
time at all, as monkeys are very good mimics,
they start picking fruit from the trees to throw
back at you and before long you have all the
fruit you need, you can fill your basket and go
home! The secret is to throw oranges at the
monkeys!

You will say, 'What on earth is all that
about? As though we could go to a forest and
throw oranges over the wall at the monkeys!'
But it is an image. Have you never seen someone
sowing seed in a field? He is throwing oranges at
the monkeys, only, in this case, the oranges are
minute and the monkeys are hidden under the
surface of the soil. When the sower has finished
he can go away in peace of mind, and when he
comes back a few months later, he only has to
reap the harvest and fill his granary.

'Oh, all right,' you may say, 'if that's all it is,
we have understood.' I doubt it. You still have
not interpreted it correctly. The monkeys are the
forces of nature, whether under the soil or in the
trees makes no difference. It is a symbol. And
now for the explanation : the universe created by
God is an immense forest bursting with treasures. The walls are all the obstacles which pre-

vent men from reaching those treasures. The monkeys are the entities of the hidden world and the oranges are the light and love that you decide to spread all round you by means of your thoughts and feelings. And then what happens? Well, once you start throwing your oranges, the entities of the Invisible World do the same, they send you fruit from the forest trees, that is to say, blessings of all kinds, and they send you a hundredfold what you send others. But if you throw hatred, bitterness and anger, then, one day, that is what will be thrown back at you.

'As you sow so shall you reap', and this also means that what you do today directly prepares your future. At every instant by your inner attitude you can give direction to your future. Every decision you make, whether for good or ill, sets the course of your future whether for good or for ill.

Just suppose that today you decide to serve God, to help your fellow men, to overcome the bad influence of your lower self: at once, your future becomes beautiful, full of light and power. All the marvels of creation are in store for you. Why are you unable to experience them at once? Because the past still has a hold on you. But if you work faithfully, always maintaining the same decision, always heading in the same direction, little by little the past will be paid off

and one day you will come into your divine in-
heritance. On the other hand, if you decide to go
back to a life of selfishness everything will be
changed once again, and you will begin to store
up for yourself a different future, one of suffering
and disillusionment, even though, for the time
being, you may go on amusing yourself and putting through your business deals. Your present
life will not change all at once because you still
have some funds in reserve and you don't see the
dark future you are preparing for yourself. But
as soon as your reserves run out, that horrible
future will be upon you. It is easy to create the
future but it is very difficult to erase the past.

Let me illustrate this with another example:
suppose you feel like taking a trip and you are
trying to choose between Nice and Moscow.
Let's say you decide to go to Nice. From then on
your itinerary is predetermined: the countryside
you see on your way, your fellow-passengers, the
stations the train goes through are all decided in
advance. Once you choose your destination you
have to follow the itinerary which already exists.
It is not you who create the countryside you
travel through. Its existence does not depend on
you, but what does depend on you is the initial
choice of direction.

In point of fact we do not actually create our
future. To say that man creates his own future is

a manner of speaking, it would be more exact to say that he chooses the direction he wants to go in. You say, 'I'll go that way.' All right. But it is not up to you to create the regions your route takes you through nor their inhabitants. They have long since been created by God. We do not create our evil fate, but we steer ourselves towards its treacherous quicksands, swamps and forests full of dangers. We decide only what direction we shall take, that is all. And if, on the other hand, we choose to go in the direction of a splendid future, the same rules apply: we decide to go in that direction but the future is already there, waiting for us. There are thousands of different regions and spheres in space, peopled with an infinite variety of creatures, and according to the region we choose as our goal, our path will lead us upwards or downwards until we reach it.

Every kind of distress and every kind of happiness exist already and others have experienced them before us. They were created long, long ago, but it is up to us now, to choose between them. And that is why, at this very moment, you must decide to change your course and steer towards the Heavenly regions which God has prepared for you from all eternity.

2

YOU WILL SEPARATE THE SUBTLE
FROM THE GROSS

From childhood, most human beings know that when they want to eat something, fruit, fish, oysters or snails, they have to start by separating the edible parts from the skin and bones, or from the core, pips or shell. When they eat cheese, they automatically leave the crust; they are conscious of the need to eliminate harmful or indigestible elements from their food. In fact they have even invented all kinds of methods designed to do just that: refining, sterilization, pasteurization, etc.

This custom of peeling, separating and rejecting from their food anything dirty or not fit for consumption, is a tremendous step in the evolutionary process which raises man above the animals. The only trouble is that men still have not understood that there are other areas where they should also clean, wash and eliminate, sort out and separate what is valuable from what is worthless, the pure from the impure. On the level of feelings and thoughts, for instance, they are constantly absorbing and digesting a different kind of food, but in this area they are still like cats: they swallow the whole mouse including the skin and the guts! In other words, they absorb everything, even what is dirty and harmful. They still have to learn to sort out the good from the bad in their psychic food, as they have learned to do for their physical food.

It is written in the Emerald Tablet of Hermes Trismegistus, 'You shall separate the subtle from the gross', which means that you must separate the pure from the impure. Of course, Hermes Trismegistus was not talking about food, even spiritual food, he was talking about the Philosopher's Stone. But still, the same principle applies. What is pure must be separated from what is impure, just as gold and precious stones have to be separated from their matrix. In fact, the whole of life, all industries and trades are based on the principle of separating or sorting things. Wherever you go in shops and supermarkets, in the diamond and gem trades – things are always being sorted. Exams and competitions are ways of sorting too, whether it be a question of choosing a Commander-in-Chief or this year's Miss World, there is always some sorting and eliminating to be done! But no one seems to realize that in the spiritual life too one has to sort and separate, choose and eliminate. If you ask people, even well-educated people, which are the harmful thoughts and feelings which cause disease and disintegration in man, they simply do not know. To them, all thoughts and feelings seem to be about the same. They never imagine that here, too, there are distinctions to be made, just as with foods or fuels which are classed according to their quality.

In the past, people used to light and heat their homes with very poor quality fuels which smoked and made one's eyes smart, and smelt so awful one almost suffocated! Nowadays, we use electricity which leaves no waste and produces no smoke. For coal, we now know that there are different qualities, ranging from the kind that gives very little heat and leaves a lot of slag, to that which gives a great deal of heat and leaves very little waste. No matter what kind of fuel you use: coal, wood, oil, petrol or straw, it always contains a certain amount of non-combustible material, but in different proportions, and it is this proportion that is interesting. Every material can be classed according to its quality, as better or less good, and that is why we always have to choose and discriminate. And the same applies to our feelings.

Feelings can be compared to fuels, and as they are not all top quality, they do not all provide the best source of light or heat or motive power. Just as for food, some feelings are 'edible' while others must be rejected because they contain some slag or dirt which the astral 'stomach' would be unable to digest. Let's suppose that you are in a rage, a prey to feelings of jealousy, hatred and revenge. What happens? Well, there will certainly be a lot of heat, but there will also be a lot of smoke and a lot of waste which will poison you. You should know this! Of course, there is no branch of approved science which studies humans' feelings with a view to classing them. Any old feeling is good enough. Down it goes like a dainty morsel and no one bothers to wonder what effect it will have on them. And it is exactly the same with our thoughts: no one discriminates between what is beneficial and what is harmful; there is no scale of values by which to judge them.

All those who believe they should allow even the most licentious passions or desires to express themselves without inhibition are in reality ignoramuses who have never studied human beings and who do not have the first idea about how they were created to start with. All they know is that they have stomachs and sexual organs which, obviously, have to be catered to! I agree. They must be catered for, but should we not be a little more discriminating all the same?

Of course, young people will say, 'No, no. No discrimination,' but since they accept that they have to discriminate in what they eat, why should they not accept that if they swallow any and every feeling or pleasure without discrimination they will make themselves ill?

Men eat bread, fruit, vegetables, fish, meat, etc., and in the area of feelings, there is as much variety and as many rich foods as in the physical sphere. Some feelings are like pork-butcher's meat: black-pudding and smoked ham, whereas others are wines or fruit or vegetables. But as human beings know nothing about the world of feelings, they eat whatever takes their fancy and then they fall ill. They must learn not to eat food which poisons them; such things as anger, spite and jealousy and, above all, sensual love, for that kind of love contains a lot of toxic elements.

Wherever you go you will find that men have countless wants and desires in their hearts. That is one commodity that is never in short supply in the world! But what is in short supply – in fact it is so rare as to be almost non-existent – is the wisdom that would enable men to choose amongst all their desires and to satisfy only those which would not hinder their true development. Although this wisdom is the most precious thing anyone could ever possess, no one wants it. No one seeks it. Why? Because their reasoning is faulty. They think that being wise means giving up certains joys and pleasures, and they have no wish to deprive themselves. This thinking is equivalent to admitting that they are both ignorant and stupid because, in reality, they would be far happier if they had enough wisdom to discern the true nature of their feelings and to sort out the good from the bad. How can they be happy if they are blind? When you cannot see, you cannot take precautions to protect yourself and you are at the mercy of whatever you bump into. Don't imagine that blindness will bring you happiness! It is as though someone handed you a closed bag, full of all kinds of things, saying, 'Go ahead, reach in and take whatever you like.' Without looking to see what is in there you put in your hand and get bitten to death by a snake! Believe me, if you are blind, there will always be a snake to bite you.

Over and above the physical body, man has other more subtle bodies: etheric, astral, mental, causal, buddhic and atmic. When he gives free rein to his passions he stirs up currents on the astral plane, thereby releasing the monstrous entities which dwell there and, without realizing it, attracts them to come and invade humanity. Man is totally ignorant of his own structure and composition, and of the constant interaction that goes on between human beings and the invisible beings in the other regions of the universe. It is this ignorance which is the cause of all his misfortunes. Whereas the disciple who knows how he has been put together in the Lord's workshops and how he is in constant relationship with the inhabitants of other planes of the universe, becomes aware of the need to pick and choose: he eliminates certain elements, closing his doors to hostile forces and opening them to forces which are beneficial, harmonious and constructive.

My dear brothers and sisters, you must realize that your bodies are composed of the ingredients you absorb and, therefore, if these are impure, you will be impure, if they are harmful, you will fall ill. This is an absolute law, not only on the physical plane but also on the psychic or spiritual plane. Just as you have to be careful to eat food that has been properly cleaned and washed, in the same way, on the level of your thoughts and feelings, you have to be on guard night and day against intruders.

Every country puts customs officers at its ports of entry to check on who goes in and out. If you have no customs officers to stop dangerous, ill-intentioned visitors from entering your territory, you will be invaded by entities from every region and you will be contaminated. Put customs men at your ports of entry and each time a thought turns up and wants to come in, say, 'Wait a minute: where are you from? Show me your colours. What will you bring in with you if I let you in?' In this way you would foresee the catastrophic results of admitting certain thoughts and send them packing.

There is a science to sorting the good from the bad. Thoughts and feelings are not all made of the same materials, there are degrees of purity, and the higher you go to find your materials, the purer they will be. In fact, you can see this, too, on the physical plane: pure materials are lighter and have a tendency to rise, whereas all that is impure is heavy and settles like dregs and mud on the bottom. Also, the purer your materials, the better will they resist wear and tear. This is why you must build your body of the purest materials so as to be able to resist suffering and even death, for if the materials you use are of the very highest quality, suffering and death have no power over them. Disease and death have power only if they can get a hold on something. Even the Devil has no power over you unless he can find weaknesses or vices to hold on to, in other words, unless he finds impure materials in you. If man is afflicted with so many distressing circumstances in his life, it is because he allows the forces of evil to get a hold on him and penetrate inside.

I have told you that I do not read too many books because the greatest truths in life are not to be found in books written by men, but in the great book of Nature. Everything has been written in that book, and what I am telling you now is drawn from the lessons I have learned from insects: cockroaches, ants, fleas, etc. When a house is very clean, insects are no problem, but as soon as you leave a little dirt about or some remnants of food which begin to rot, then the insects arrive. How do they know there is something for them to eat? And why are some people bitten by fleas and lice and not others? Because their blood contains impurities which provide excellent food for these little beasties. They only like what is impure; purity has no attraction for them!

If you have no desire to be invaded by cockroaches or ants, keep your house clean, if you have no desire to be bitten by fleas, purify your bloodstream, and if you don't want to be invaded by harmful spirits, be sure not to prepare food for them. The Gospels recount some instances of people possessed by devils. Why had the devils entered them? Because they found in them the kind of impure nourishment they thrive on. And this is why Jesus, when he chased the devils out, said to the person he had just saved, 'Go and sin no more.' In other words, 'Don't let any impurities into you again.'

It is important for man's health and beauty and even for his intelligence that he choose his physical food well, and it is equally important that he choose his spiritual food wisely. His whole future depends on it. It is the quality of what he absorbs that will make him either a superior being or a brute and a criminal.

3

EVOLUTION AND CREATION

From the very first stages of his evolution, man has manifested the urge to create, as we can see from archeological discoveries dating back to the most primitive civilizations. In the same way, from a very early age, children always have the urge to build, draw, paint pictures, etc. One could say that this need to be a creator, and in this to resemble his Heavenly Father, is one of man's strongest and most constant instincts.

Art in all its forms is proof that this urge to create, which is common to all human beings, is not restricted to the creation of children, to biological reproduction with a view to ensuring the preservation of the species. The existence of art demonstrates man's need to go beyond himself, to reach towards something more beautiful, subtler and more perfect. Man's creative faculties lie on a higher plane than his ordinary level of consciousness. They dwell in a region of his soul which manifests itself as a capacity to explore and contemplate and, finally, to capture the elements of a reality which far surpasses him. To create is to surpass and outstrip one's own limitations.

The reason why certain inventors, for instance, have been able to make such revolutionary discoveries, is that they were able to rise to the realm of imagination and higher still, to that of intuition, and tune in to ideas and images which they then retranscribed and materialized. Modern science has not yet explored the possibilities open to intuition which, like radar or some kind of cosmic radiolocator, can foresee, predict and tune in to the future. From time to time, when a thinker who takes a stand half-way between orthodox science and esoteric science, launches new ideas, no one takes him seriously. He is criticized or ridiculed and only later does it become evident that he was one of humanity's pioneers.

Man's imaginative power is a truly creative faculty and if he learns to purify and cultivate it in perfect clarity and lucidity, it is capable of opening his eyes to realities which he has never dreamt of. All inventors spend long hours plunged in research and meditation and it is undeniable that their intuition is an authentic faculty. Here, in this Initiatic School, we are doing exactly what they do, but consciously, in full awareness of what we are doing. The difference is that our imagination is not aimed at physical, chemical or technical discoveries, but at inner, spiritual discoveries. And we too can discover wonderful things whose existence many people never even suspect.

As I have already explained, imagination is like the spouse of the inner man, who gives birth to his children. Some of his offspring are a great success and some are a disaster, according to the quality of the seed he supplied. And if his children make mischief and cause damage to property it is the father who is held responsible, it is he who will have to pay a fine, who is liable to be tried and condemned to pay damages in their place. On the other hand, when they win prizes or competitions, it is their father who receives the credit! You will propably say, 'But what children are you talking about?' I am talking about our thoughts and feelings. They are our children, each one of us has fathered any number of them. This is a very vast field for study and analysis. But I must not digress; let us get back to the heart of the subject.

This creative instinct, therefore, which we all have, incites us to reach beyond the limits of our ordinary capacities and puts us in touch with other regions, other worlds filled with subtle, luminous, etheric beings. And it is thanks to that part of ourselves which has gone out from us and reached higher planes where it tunes in to entire-

ly new elements, that we are able to create children who are superior to us, or works of art
which surpass our limits. Very often, a creation
is far more beautiful than its creator. Sometimes
one sees a funny little man who looks like nothing on earth and one is utterly astonished to discover that he has created some tremendous work
of art, worthy of a giant! That subtle part of
himself which is capable of travelling very far
and very high, has gone out from him and gath-
ered a rich harvest of new elements and when
later, he sets to work, he produces something
prodigious, something entirely original which
fills the whole world with admiration.

Although all men have the creative urge, unfortunately very few are capable of becoming
true creators on a spiritual plane, very few rise
to this level and realize that, in order to produce
sublime works of art, they must know certain
laws and apply certain methods. What these
methods are you will soon understand.

How is it that, in winter, the earth is so
dingy, bare and sterile whereas when spring
comes it is clothed in lovely colourful vegeta-
tion: grasses, flowers, trees and fruits? The reason is simply that with the coming of spring the
earth receives more sunlight and with the sunlight come certain elements lacking in winter. So
she sets to work and surpasses herself, producing

extraordinary, brightly-coloured works of art and regaling us with the nectars and perfumes she offers to all creatures. If man wants to create and produce anything noteworthy, therefore, he must take a leaf out of nature's book and find a 'sun', a being more powerful and more intelligent than himself with whom to unite and interrelate.

Now do you see why we go up to see the sunrise in the morning? It is in order to create works which resemble him, works which will be ever new, transparent, full of light, warmth and life. But, in fact, the sun, in this context, is a symbol : a symbol of God Himself to Whom we turn in order to unite ourselves with Him, for it is thanks to our interrelation with the Lord that we shall become creators like Him. Here you have the fundamental reason, the true motive for prayer, meditation and contemplation and all the spiritual exercices. But I am not sure that all this is very clear in your minds, so I shall try to explain it more fully.

For a long time now I have had a burning desire to declare war on the materialistic philosophy of today – to declare war on it and wipe it off the face of the earth! 'What ambition!' you will say; 'What pride! No one has ever managed to do it so far.' Well, I know that. You're right, of course. But I have a few very simple arguments of my own and I believe that with their help I shall succeed where others have failed! First I take two glasses into which I pour two different perfumes. The glasses remain separate, they are two quite distinct objects. From a materialistic point of view there is no communication between them, and this is perfectly true on the material level. Seen as exterior forms, as containers and nothing more, the two glasses are quite separate. But this is no longer true if you consider their contents, for each perfume gives off some subtle particles which rise and spread into the air and intermingle. Any science which concerns itself exclusively with tangible, visible and measurable phenomena knows nothing of what goes on, on the much more subtle level of invisible emanations and quintessences, and so, on this level, its conclusions cease to be true and reliable. Half the truth escapes it.

Now, let's consider the sun: he is very far away, millions of miles away from us and yet we can feel his presence here on earth. He touches us, he warms and heals us. How can he be so close in spite of the distance that lies between him and the earth? It is because something goes out from him, a quintessence which is part of him: his rays. And by means of his rays he establishes the contact. When he embraces us, caresses and penetrates us we become one with him. And since the light and warmth of the sun are none other than the sun himself, we can say that the sun and the earth touch, that the planets touch each other. Take our planet: there is the earth, the soil, and over the earth there is water. Over the water is the air, and above the air is the ether. It is on this level that one can say that the planets touch each other. They are not in contact on the physical, solid level, but on the subtler level of the soul. And this is why astrologers have always believed in the influence of the planets and constellations on men's lives.

Now, let us look at those miniature planets and constellations: men and women. What happens between them? What happens between a boy and a girl when they see each other for the first time and experience a mutual attraction from a distance? From a purely materialistic point of view, we have here two distinct and separate physical entities and there is no contact between them and therefore no communication. But if you look at the scene from the point of view of one who believes in the spirit, it is quite obvious to you that that is nonsense: the souls of these two young people are in communication with each other. They are really and truly fused into one by means of their subtle fluids and emanations, in exactly the same way as the rays of two suns in space blend and fuse together.

Perhaps these few words will help you to understand how, by means of his subtle bodies, man is able to reach out to the Universal Soul and blend with it. This is the reason for prayer. Prayer is nothing more nor less than an interaction between man and his Creator, an act by which we rise above ourselves in the endeavour to find elements that will help us to create perfect, divine works. And here again we have an essential element of the cosmic moral law: if an artist wishes to create an unforgettable masterpiece which will last forever, he must take care not to restrict himself to the level of his five senses, as so many contemporary artists do. Nowadays it has become the fashion in the art world to portray the most prosaic and commonplace subjects. Most artists no longer know how to rise above themselves in order to contemplate sublime beauty. They offer their public monstrosities, gargoyles! They have lost the secret of true creativity.

If you aspire to becoming an authentic creator, you must establish contact with the Godhead in order to receive divine particles which you can then incorporate into your creation and, in this way, your child or your work of art will surpass you in beauty and intelligence. So, there you are, dear brothers and sisters, new horizons are being opened up to you: how to establish a link and an interaction between yourself and all those beings who surpass you; how to use prayer, meditation and contemplation as a means of creation. There is such a wealth of possibilities in this area that a whole existence would not be enough to explore them all.

Nothing is more important for man than to restore the bonds with his Creator. Haven't you ever realized that the conception of a child is based on the same law: the mother has to be united with the father, become one with him? All creation requires that there be union between a father and a mother. But if the subtler factor, the soul or the imagination, takes no part in the conception, then the higher elements cannot be captured and utilized and the act of creation will fail, or if it does not actually fail, its product will certainly never be better than the parents. Creation is not something stagnant, simply a reproduction or copy of something that already exists. It is a step forward, an evolutionary step. This is how each individual advances. In fact, this is how the whole cosmos advances and evolves: thanks to the creative instinct. And with the exception of God Himself, everything must evolve.

4

TWO JUSTICES:
HUMAN AND DIVINE

I

For centuries men have understood that life in society is based on the law of exchange. Experience has taught them that life could be maintained only on condition that each individual takes and gives, gives and takes, and that this applies on all levels of life : physical, psychological and spiritual. This law of exchange is called justice : you take something for yourself and you give its equivalent in exchange. If you can maintain a right balance between what you take and what you give, then you are just.

But people do not bother their heads too much about giving or paying exactly what they owe : they take a lot and they give very little. What they do not realize is that their debts accumulate and are recorded on that tiny tape recorder we all have within us and which records everything we do. One day they will have to pay and this will involve suffering for them. They have eaten and drunk to excess, stolen and abused the love of those they have seduced or betrayed, and then, because they have managed to get away without paying the bill, they imagine they will never be caught. And this is where they are making a big mistake. It makes no difference if they change their name and address and even their nationality, the Lords of Karma who dwell on high have a record of their prints and can trace them. In fact, very often in the same incarnation, they find the culprit, present the bill and demand payment. Much of the suffering endured by men is simply payment for injustices they have committed.

Justice should be understood as liberation, for only when you have given back or paid for what you have taken are you free. And this is why, at this point, I want to help you to understand the justice which should characterize our relations with our family, with society and nature, and even with the whole cosmos.

Man receives a great deal from his parents: his body and life itself. (Let's say, for the sake of argument, that he receives life from them, although in fact, they have not created him but simply transmitted life to him). He receives clothes, food, a home, an education. This means that a considerable debt has accumulated and must be paid. Many children refuse to acknowledge this, they criticize their parents and openly oppose them. Some even detest them. This is unjust. Their parents have loved them and suffered for them, they have fed, clothed and protected them, nursed them through illnesses and given them an education. So, before anything else, man has a debt towards his parents.

But then man also has a debt towards the society or nation he belongs to, for it has given him a rich heritage of culture and civilization, with schools, museums, libraries, laboratories, theatres, etc. And society puts all kinds of things at his disposal: trains, ships, airplanes, doctors to take care of him, teachers and professors to instruct him, an army and even a police force to protect him! Then he also owes something to his race, for it has given him not only the colour of his skin but a whole physical and psychological structure – a mentality. But this is not all: he also has a debt to the earth which gave him birth and nourished him with her fruits, to our solar system (because it is thanks to the sun and the planets that we are continually sustained and vivified), to the whole universe and, finally, to God.

How many people realize that they have never done anything but take, take, take and that now they have a huge debt to pay? Ah, according to them, they owe nothing to anybody. In fact, not only do they think they owe nothing,

but they also think they have the right to criticize and demolish anything and everything.
What a deplorable mentality! What they do not
know is that if they go on like that, they will be
wiped off the face of the earth, for Nature cannot
tolerate creatures who do not respect her laws:
they are a threat to the whole and, in one way or
another, she gets rid of them.

A disciple who understands the importance
of the law of Justice loves, first and foremost, his
parents and, in order to repay his debt to them,
he is careful to do only what is right and good for
them. But he also repays his debt to society, his
country, the whole of mankind, the universe
and, finally, to God Himself. And the coin with
which he pays his debts is his work, his thoughts
and feelings and a grateful heart. Through his
activity he is continually communicating something positive and good to the whole universe.
This is how man pays his debts and Nature ac-
knowledges the intelligence of such a being. But
what about all those who don't pay their debts?
Nature regards them as thieves, dishonest, unjust creatures who need to be taught a lesson; so
she chastises them in order to make them wiser
and better.

To be just, therefore, is first and foremost to
understand that there are certain laws and that
when we take anything from Nature, whether it

is food, air, water, warmth or the sun's rays, we incur a debt. And as we cannot pay this debt with money, we must pay with love, gratitude and respect and with a will to learn what is written in her book. We pay our debt to Nature, too, when we do something good for another creature, when we communicate a little light and warmth to others. Suppose you have a Master who has given you untold treasures: what exactly do you owe him? You cannot pay him in kind, with advice, instruction or consolation. He does not need that from you. It is not he who must be the beneficiary of your good deeds, but others. If you pass on to other human beings the treasures you have received from your Master he will be delighted and consider himself repaid in full.

We are not obliged to give back the air we breathe or the water we drink in the form of air and water. How could we go about manufacturing air or water, or the warmth and light of the sun's rays? We have received our bodies from the earth and one day, it is true, we are going to have to give them back. There is no other way. But in the meantime, as long as we are still living, we are entitled to keep and use them. No one asks us to give them back. What we can give is light, for man has been constructed in such a way that he is capable of radiating, shining and sending out rays of light into the whole universe. He has received a quintessence of light which he can continually amplify, vivify and send out into space. But he can do so only on condition that he really works at it and practises, otherwise all that comes out of him is darkness.

I realize that all this is new for you, but remember this: although we are severely limited on the physical plane, on the spiritual plane our possibilities are infinite and we can give what we receive a hundredfold.

You may say that no one has ever explained justice to you in this way before. I know. Human justice is limited to the cases of murder, theft or divorce that come up before the courts. But divine justice is quite another matter and it is this, the only true justice, that you need to understand. When, for example, you see that someone detests you, there must be a reason. Try and find out what it is. Perhaps you owe him a debt. Why not try to pay off your debt by doing something for him, either on the physical or on the spiritual plane? If you want to free yourself more rapidly you will have to choose the way of divine justice, the way of kindness, generosity, love and self-sacrifice. In this way, long-standing debts that would take years or even centuries to pay off in other ways, can be paid in full very quickly and, sometimes, instantaneously.

This is why there are people who have accepted to suffer persecution, martyrdom and death : in order to free themselves by paying off the debts accumulated from other incarnations. Those who are truly enlightened choose the quickest route. They are in a hurry and have no desire to lag behind in the lower regions as miserable captives for longer than necessary. They want to be free and so they accept to suffer.

Of course there are not a great many like this. The majority try to get out of paying their debts, still thinking they can avoid them altogether if they are sly enough. Only, there you are! Karmic law always catches up with them in the end and obliges them to pay. I know that many of you, listening to me today, will stop up your ears. But the day will come when they will be crushed under the weight of their debts and then they will acknowledge the truth of what I am saying and make up their minds to tot up their own bill, how much they owe and to whom, and to pay it in one form or another. If it is too late to repay their father, for instance, then they can pay their own son or their wife.

Well, there you have the disciple's task : to honour all his debts and obligations from now on, and even to pay more than he owes in order to free himself more rapidly. So now I suggest that you work at this for the next few days : re-

view your whole life and try to remember how
you have behaved, what you have taken without
giving in exchange, and from whom. Then, go
and find those people, apologize to them and
pay them what you owe them or do something
for them, saying, 'I didn't realize. I was blind.
Please forgive me if I made mistakes and accept
this or that so that we can be at peace with each
other.'

And what if you cannot find the people you
owe something to because they are no longer on
earth? Then you can turn directly to God, saying, 'Lord, I understand now for the first time,
how unjust I've been with others. I've cheated
them and imposed upon them. Now it's too late.
I can't make up to them for the wrong I did
them, but I do want to advance, to make progress. So, please, Lord, here is my life. Take it.
From now on it will be consecrated to your service. It's the most precious thing I possess and I
want you to dispose of it to pay all my debts.
You know far better than I who my creditors are
and how much I owe them. I'm at your service
for all eternity.' This is the best possible way to
put everything right. When the Lord sees that
you have reached such a high level of consciousness as to want to consecrate your life to Him for
all Eternity (and be sure to make it quite clear
that it is for Eternity and not just for this incar-

nation), He will be astounded at all the light that flows from you. He knows very well that if you can feel and say such a thing it means that you are full of light and He is dazzled! And of course, as He does not want to be outdone by you, He shows Himself to be even more generous and wipes out many of your debts, 'There, it's finished. Paid in full. We won't talk about it any more. Now go and work hard.'

For years, when I was young, I implored the powers above to come to my help, 'What can I do? I'm weak, stupid, ordinary, worthless; do you really want me to stay that way? I can't be of any use to you like this. I warn you, you'll have cause to regret it if you don't help me, so hurry up and take everything I have. Take my life, if you want, and come and live in me. I can't go on like this. Send me angels. Send me quantities of noble and intelligent beings, full of light and purity. It will be to your advantage. Otherwise I'll only make mistakes and it will be all your fault, because you didn't come and help me when I asked you to.' You see? I threatened them! And upstairs, they scratched their heads and said, 'Well, of all things! He's really got us in a tight spot.' So they discussed it and decided that if they left me as I was, it was quite true, I would only cause a lot of trouble and do a lot of damage, and they decided to give me what I asked for. And now it seems that from time to time, I manage to do something which is not entirely reprehensible!

And now, what about you? Why not make the same request? What are you waiting for? Go ahead and ask. Ah, yes, I know. You are afraid to consecrate your life to God: you want to keep it for yourself. How often have I heard people say, 'I am going to live my own life.' That is all well and good, but what kind of life are you going to live, stupid or divine? Everyone wants to 'live his own life', and it usually means a life without rhyme or reason.

From now on you should aim at something better. Say, 'Lord, I'm beginning to realize that without You, without Your light and intelligence, I'm worthless: I'm ashamed, disgusted and sick of myself and I'm ready to serve You and to do something for Your children and for the whole world.' Repeat this day and night. Even if the Lord stops up His ears because He is tired of listening to you, never stop! The twenty-four Lords of Karma will hold a meeting (I know these meetings and I know the Chairman too, He is an extraordinary, sublime being). They will hold their meeting and as you are continually pestering them with your plea, they will publish a decree to be proclaimed throughout all the regions of space, declaring that from such and such a date, at such and such a time, a change will take place in your life. Then the Angels and all the faithful servants of God will set to work at once to apply this decree and, sure enough, you will see that something really does change in your destiny.

II

Most people have not yet attained mastery over their own impulses. If they have been disappointed by someone, they do all they can to destroy his reputation and make life unbearable for him. If he falls ill or even attempts suicide, they never stop to wonder if it is their fault. It never occurs to them that the Powers on high might hold them responsible for their enemy's misfortunes and that they are preparing a terrible Karma for themselves.

Even if you have been cheated or disappointed by someone this does not give you the right to go about telling everyone what he has done. You may say, 'But I'm only doing it to set the record straight. It's a question of justice!' This is where you are mistaken. That notion of justice is the source of all your misfortunes. Everybody seems to think he has the right to punish others and teach them a lesson in the name of justice! Leave justice out of it! But then perhaps you will ask, 'Well, in that case what should I do?'

I'll tell you : you should have recourse to a principle which is above justice, a principle of love, kindness and generosity.

It is already two thousand years since Jesus gave us this new doctrine of love and, in spite of it, Christians still apply the law of Moses : an eye for an eye and a tooth for a tooth. They still have not understood that if they want to become truly noble and free they will have to stop applying that antiquated notion of justice. Do you think you will feel triumphant if you see your enemy completely ruined? It is more than probable that you will not feel particularly proud of yourself and will begin to be sorry for what you did. But by then it will be too late and you will have prepared very hard times for yourself, in this incarnation or in the next.

You must learn to adopt a totally different attitude. Let's suppose that you have done someone a kindness, lent him some money, for instance, and then, one day, you find that he does not deserve all you have done for him and you go and tell everybody about your generosity and his supposed unworthiness. Why do you have to talk about it? If you do something good and then go and tell everyone about it, you are undoing all the good you did. It was ordained on high that you were to be rewarded but then you go and spoil it all by erasing your good deed.

Even if someone cheats you and does you an injury, it does not matter. Never talk about it. On the contrary, your whole attitude should show that person that you are better than he is. One day he will end by being ashamed of himself and not only will he do everything in his power to right the wrong he did you, but he will take you as his model. When are you going to make up your minds to behave with high-mindedness and generosity? You must learn to close your eyes to some things and to forgive. This is the only way to grow and become a truly noble being. If you learn to do this, even the things you have lost will be given back to you a hundred-fold. Otherwise, if you try to revenge yourself, you create so many negative forces that one day they will strike back and it is you who will be submerged by them. When this happens you will perhaps understand that you have behaved like an imbecile! Whatever anyone does to you therefore, never try to get your own back. Wait for Heaven to pass judgment in your favour, for this it will inevitably do if your behaviour is above reproach.

I think you should begin to realize how very useful it is to receive the light of Initiatic Science. When the average man who knows nothing of this is wronged or offended by someone, obviously he responds by teaching him a lesson – so-called – and everyone thinks that this response is only normal and just. Well, perhaps it is justice in the eyes of the crowd but as I have already explained, justice as it is understood by the common man is simply stupidity in the eyes of an Initiate. For look what happens next: since this man has acted on his desire for revenge, he is automatically caught up in a vicious circle from which there is no escape. He has got rid of one enemy: true! But there will always be others to take his place and he will have to try and get rid of them. In other words, he has put himself in the position of having to foster negative feelings and attitudes which can only strengthen his lower nature, and in the end, what will he have gained? Absolutely nothing! For all those enemies he has massacred are going to come back. They have never really ceased to exist. They will reincarnate and one day it will be their turn to revenge themselves. And this is how anyone who thinks he can get rid of his opponents is, in reality, only preparing others for the future and, in the end, it is he who will go under.

This old method of revenge is no solution. On the contrary, it complicates things, burdens a man's existence and increases his Karmic debt. In the long run it leads to his downfall and eventual elimination. No one can pretend that in seeking revenge, man is obeying the dictates of a sublime intelligence!

In contrast, take the case of a true Initiate. He too has been outraged and defiled, trodden under, wronged and humiliated by enemies. But as he knows the law, he responds with other methods. Instead of revenging himself directly on his adversaries he leaves them strictly alone: they are free to develop in whatever way they want and, secure in the knowledge of how they will end up, he uses his time to prepare himself. What is he getting ready for? To massacre them? No! I have already explained that he refuses to assume a debt towards them, he intends to maintain his freedom and develop his power. And power does not mean getting your gun and shooting your enemy. That is not power, but weakness and ignorance besides!

An Initiate gets ready in a different way. He says, 'Aha, you thought you'd wiped me out, eh? Just you wait. You're in for a surprise!' And he sets to work to pursue a stupendous work of inner transformations. He prays and meditates, studies and practises until one day, he has acquired true wisdom and true power. And if, when this is done, he meets his old enemies again, they are dumbfounded. Something indescribable begins to happen in their minds and hearts and souls. Seeing the light that flows from

the Initiate who, instead of wasting his time trying to get even with them, has been working on
his own transformation, they feel tarnished and
deformed. They begin to realize that they have
been wasting their life and decide to change.
And lo and behold, here is the Initiate's true
triumph, his true victory: without so much as
laying a finger on them, simply by leaving them
alone, he has gained the upper hand over his
enemies.

In Bulgaria we have a saying, 'No need to
push a drunkard, he'll fall over by himself.' And
it is quite true. Someone who is drunk with pride
and self-sufficiency, who is intoxicated with his
own grandeur, will fall over all by himself one
day, without any assistance from you! If you
push him, the law will hold you responsible for
his fall, but if you leave him alone he will inevitably fall over and it will not be on your conscience. In the meantime, you will have been
busy improving yourself, concerned only with
things pure, luminous and divine. Isn't this by
far the best solution? Of course it is! It is a
method which demands a great deal of love,
kindness, patience and light, but for my part I
know of none better. Without ill will, without
vindictiveness of any kind, you will heap coals
of fire on the heads of your enemies: they will
see what you have become and that will be

enough for them. They will regret their behaviour and come and make reparation for the
wrong they did you.

For there is, after all, a natural law according
to which anyone who has done you wrong will
be obliged, one day or another, in this life or in a
future incarnation, to come and find you and
make amends. When this happens, you may feel
intuitively that they are old enemies and you
may try to keep them at a distance. This will not
make any difference. They will keep coming
back and insisting that you accept their offers of
help. This is the law, and it has already proved
true for many of you. Everybody who has ever
wronged you and whom you have not wronged
in return is obliged by the law to come and make
amends to you, whether he likes it or not. His
opinion is of no importance.

An Initiate is capable of revenge therefore,
but only with the weapons of light and love. And
you, too, can revenge yourselves. It is normal to
revenge oneself. Why not? But there are two
ways of doing it: the first is to knock out your
enemy and tear him apart; the second is to leave
him intact but to induce a radical change in his
heart and soul which can only be beneficial both
to him and to you. The second way is twice as
good as the first.

I most sincerely advise all the members of the Brotherhood therefore, to do everything in their power to settle their conflicts without creating more Karma for themselves. Why is it that even members of the same family have to go to court to settle their disputes over money? When are they going to learn to be above such methods? Why do humans always cling to their interests and their possessions? If they could just make one little gesture, they would find freedom! They might not feel free immediately of course, in fact they might be a bit ill at ease and even suffer from it to begin with, but if they can bring themselves to make a gesture of disinterested-ness and abnegation they will soon discover new dimensions, a new light, and none will be proud-er or happier than they, because they will have achieved something very difficult : a victory over their lower nature or personality.

It is your personality, your lower self, which is always urging you to grab the lion's share, to take your revenge, to slander others and take them to court. And with it all you believe you have understood the Teaching! Let me disillu-sion you. Those who behave like that have not understood the first thing about the Teaching. They listen to the lectures and read the books and exclaim in admiration ; and then they go on behaving exactly as they have always done. Do not think for a moment that I am blind to all that. It is really pitiful: how can they go on behaving like everybody else when they have been privileged to witness so much light, when so many tremendous truths have been revealed to them?

If you count on divine love, wisdom and generosity to help you solve all your problems you will never be alone because you will have forged a bond with Heaven. And here again is a point that many of you have still not understood. You still do not really believe and trust sufficiently in the power of the Invisible World to sustain you and smooth out your path if you apply its methods. You are always only too ready to trust in all the intrigues and deceits suggested by your personalities. And this is why you never really succeed in any of your enterprises: sooner or later the Invisible World bars your way. Whereas Initiates and those who respect the laws and count on Heaven to help them are never abandoned, even if the whole world forsakes them, they are sustained, encouraged and enlightened and in the long run, they always triumph.

III

So you intend to revenge yourself on someone who has done you an injury, is that it? Very
well. For the sake of argument, let's say that you
are entitled to do so, but let me ask you one
thing: do you know for certain exactly what
punishment he deserves? Perhaps you will say,
'Yes. It's perfectly simple: he hit me and I'm going to hit him back!' All right, but you had better think again. Can you give him *exactly* what
he gave you? Of course you can't, and all the
more so if the injury he did you is not so simple:
you can never do exactly the same harm to
someone as he has done to you. It is far better
not to get involved. Leave it to those who are capable of paying each creature his just deserts. If
not, in your ignorance you will only go and
make some silly mistake which you will have to
pay for later: in the future, you will meet this
same enemy again and your problems with him
will begin all over again.

This fact of the impossibility of rendering absolute justice is illustrated in a very original way by Shakespeare in *The Merchant of Venice*. The money-lender, Shylock, had lent Antonio, the merchant, three thousand ducats with the agreement that if the money was not repaid by a certain date he would have the right to cut a pound of flesh off Antonio's body. When the fateful day arrived, Antonio could not pay because his ship had gone down at sea taking with it his entire fortune, so Shylock took him to court charging him with not honouring his contract, and claimed his pound of flesh. Since no plea for pity could make Shylock renounce his claim, the judge reluctantly ordered Antonio to pay his debt. But then one of the judges (who was really a young woman in disguise), intervened, calling for scales to be brought. Then, telling Antonio to bare his breast, she told Shylock to take his pound of flesh, but without spilling any blood, for the contract specified only flesh. If Shylock spilled so much as one drop of blood, warned the judge, his fortune would be confiscated. Of course, Shylock was very alarmed and tried to withdraw the charge. But the judge insisted and this time she added, 'If thou tak'st more or less than a just pound... nay, if the scale do turn but in the estimation of a hair, thou diest and all thy goods are confiscate.' Shylock was even more

panic-stricken. Finally all ended well, thanks to
the wisdom of this young woman who understood how imperfect human justice was.

Even if one could calculate the exact punishment due, to be truly just one would also have to
make sure that the circumstances were the same.
Does a fine of £100 or $100 for instance, really
represent the same degree of punishment to
someone who has only that to live on as it would
to a multimillionaire? Of course not. So, you
see, it is virtually impossible to do justice. And
this is why, if you think that someone who has
wronged you fully deserves to be punished, you
should speak to the Invisible World about it.
'You see, this person did thus and so to me and,
because of that, I'm having all kinds of difficulties in such and such a way. So I'm asking you to
intervene and right this wrong.' In this way you
lodge your complaint with the heavenly courts
of justice in exactly the same way as one does in
everyday life on earth; Heaven will judge the
case and decide what to do about it. Whatever
happens, be sure not to do anything yourself.

The reason why you must do nothing is that
there is an element here which you simply cannot know, and that is that certain unpleasant
events occur in your life for certain very specific
reasons. It could be that the person you are com-
plaining about was guided in his actions by the

Invisible World in order to teach you something, so that you would understand some particular truth or even to force you to make more rapid progress. And that being so, why not use these circumstances as an occasion to work at your own development and accomplish real progress instead of ruminating all kinds of ideas of revenge, rebelling against Heaven because your enemy has not been exterminated, or taking revenge on other innocent people, as so often happens in life?

You must learn therefore to behave correctly even if others behave very badly towards you. It is not your business to punish them. There are laws in the universe to take care of that. As for you, you must avoid entertaining negative ideas because they will have a very detrimental effect on your psychic health and one day your face will reflect all the bad feelings you have nourished. You may say that you are only trying to defend your rights – perhaps. But you are still working against your own best interests and, if you persist, you will never get on to the right road.

5

THE LAW OF CORRESPONDENCES

I

The human organism is a microcosm, an exact replica of the universe, or macrocosm. Hence, between man and the universe there are points and zones which correspond and the whole of esoteric science is based on this law of correspondences. Man is infinitely small, the cosmos is infinitely vast, but between the infinitely small and the infinitely vast there is correspondence: each organ of the human body has an affinity with a given region of the cosmos. Of course, you must not think that I am saying that the cosmos has organs like ours but, in their essence, our organs and those of the cosmos have something identical in common. Thanks to the law of affinity we can establish contact with forces, centres and worlds in space which correspond to certain elements within us. A knowledge of these correspondences can open up unheard-of possibilities for us.

Between man, the microcosm, and the universe, the macrocosm, an absolute correspondence exists. But since man has destroyed that original ideal relationship with the macrocosm and with God by his disordered way of life, our task now is to restore that bond. And this is within our reach, for when man was first created, he was endowed with all he needed to evolve and develop and, in case he got lost, to find his way back to his heavenly homeland.

When a child comes into this world he has everything he needs: his heart may be a touch too far to the right, his stomach rather small or his kidneys may not function perfectly, but at least he has all the vital organs: heart, stomach, kidneys, lungs, etc. Nothing is missing. In exactly the same way, every spirit which incarnates on this earth possesses organs and faculties which correspond to all the virtues and qualities on high in Heaven and, this being so, everything is possible to him. Not all at once, of course, but gradually, if he knows and abides by the laws, he can undertake the most stupendous tasks.

What are the laws in question? Well, suppose you have two identical tuning forks: if you set one of them vibrating you will find that the other one vibrates also, without your having touched it. This is what is known as resonance. Everybody knows about this phenomenon but no one stops to analyse it and to see that exactly the same thing occurs between a human being and the cosmos. If a man attunes his physical and psychological being to the same vibrations as those of the universe, he can reach out to touch the heavenly powers and establish a bond and an interaction with them which will help and comfort him. Vibrations are a means of communication. You speak and someone hears you. You can even set certain forces in motion and draw them to yourself so that you can benefit from them. There is interaction and exchange, therefore, between you and any region of the universe you choose, and you must know that it is precisely in this interaction that God has placed man's very best means of attaining perfection.

You will ask, 'How can we attune ourselves? It's all very complicated.' No, don't worry, it will happen all by itself. If you cultivate love, selflessness, indulgence and generosity, your whole being will begin to be attuned, because you will be working with forces which automatically bring everything into harmony within you. When someone ruins his nervous system, does he do it consciously, scientifically and in all lucidity? Does he know exactly where and to what extent he is creating havoc? No, of course not! But because he entertained all kinds of outlandish thoughts and feelings, he ended by breaking down. You don't have to know exactly where all

your nerve centres are to go out of your mind!
And it is the same if you want to attune your
whole being: you simply have to entertain elevated thoughts and feelings and they will set
your spiritual centres vibrating harmoniously.

Some people who have done everything in
their power to ensure that nothing shall ever go
right for them again, spend their time moaning
that life is meaningless and that God doesn't exist. But the fact that they themselves are stupid,
ill and wretched doesn't mean that there is nobody in the whole wide world who is intelligent,
healthy and happy! It is their reasoning that is at
fault, and if they would only put that right,
everything else would improve too. So if you are
unhappy and tormented in your mind, if nothing
ever goes right for you, what should you do? Instead of standing there weeping and wringing
your hands, why not go and find someone who
can help you? 'Where are they and how can I
find them?' you ask. They are right beside you
all the time. You have only to think about them
to reach them, thanks to the law of resonance or,
as I like to call it, the law of sympathy or affinity. As soon as you know this law you are in possession of the means of rising above yourself and
of reaching out beyond your limitations to touch
the most subtle and sensitive chords of your be-

ing and set them throbbing, knowing that there are corresponding forces, entities and regions in space which will respond.

The acoustical law of resonance, the phenomenon of the echo, has often made me stop and think. You call out, 'I love you' and even if you are alone a whole host of voices reply, 'I love you, love you, love you.' If you call out, 'I hate you,' the echo sends it back to you too. And since this happens on the physical plane, why should it not happen on the mental plane also?

Or take a ball and throw it against the wall: if you forget to step aside it will bounce back and hit you. Basically the ball is obeying the same law as your voice: the law of reverberation or rebound. Here too, everyone knows this law on the physical plane but nobody believes that it applies equally on the psychological and spiritual planes. Whatever you do, good or evil, will necessarily come back to you one day. Every feeling you experience falls into a certain category and it goes out into space, awakening kindred forces which then come back to you in obedience to the law of affinity. And it is thanks to this law that man can draw on the immense reservoirs of the universe and obtain all the elements he needs just as long as he projects into space thoughts and feelings of the same breed as those he wants to attract to himself. It is the nature of your own thoughts and feelings which exactly and unfailingly determines which forces and elements you awaken and attract to yourself from outer space.

To my mind this law of affinity is the most important key, the great Arcanum, the magic wand. My whole life is based on it. Knowing this law I orient all my work in a certain direction, thinking of all that is most beautiful, all that is best for me, and then I wait for the results. Many of the things I have worked for have already come about; others will come later. I do not need to apply any other law, for this one includes them all. This law explains everything: the structure of human beings, their intelligence or stupidity, their kindness or cruelty, their fortunes and misfortunes, their wealth and their poverty – everything!

Look at what happens with fish in the ocean. The ocean contains an infinite variety of chemical elements, and one kind of fish, simply because it attracts certain elements and particles, fashions for itself a magnificent, colourful, phosphorescent body, whereas another attracts different particles and its body is dingy and ugly. Of course it is not a conscious process, but the fact remains: each fish draws from the sea those elements which correspond to its nature. This applies to us, too. We are little fish immersed in the waters of etheric ocean and, as that ocean contains all the elements provided by the Creator, we have become as we are thanks to the particular elements we have drawn from the ocean to form our bodies. Everything can be explained by this. Take the case of someone who is ugly, unhappy and always ill: his troubles do not come from his present incarnation but from previous ones, when he was neither instructed nor guided when, in his ignorance, he attracted to himself all kinds of objectionable elements and now he does not know how to get rid of them.

So be careful! You who know this law of affinity, the most potent law of magic and the foundation of the whole of creation, you must immediately set to work to attract to yourselves particles of so luminous a nature that you will begin to improve in every way. And when those you live and work with see that you have become much more friendly and radiant, that you even seem to be more intelligent and, above all, stronger and more forceful, they will begin to have a better opinion of you and your destiny will change. You see, everything in life is connected. Whereas if you are ignorant, if you do not know the laws on which all existence is based and if you are forever tearing down and destroying all that God has given you, of course, the forces of nature cannot help you for long. In the end they are obliged to leave you to your own resources. And then what sorrow and heart-break follow!

Unfortunately, so many men and women are in this state: I have personally met quantities of them. People who had no idea what they had done to get themselves into such a sorry condition, and their minds were in such chaos and obscurity that I couldn't explain anything to them. They could see no point in life, no order in the universe, nothing that made sense! To help them to understand I would have had to start from the beginning and talk to them for years on end but, above all, they would have had to be willing to listen and learn and, of course, they weren't ready to make that effort. But it is impossible to explain in five minutes the whole sequence of events that has brought someone to his present plight: where and when they had begun to go astray and how, little by little, they had brought misfortune on themselves. Unfortunately most people refuse to recognize this sequence of cause and effect in their lives. Even when it is explained to them with almost tangible arguments and proofs they still can't see it.

To my mind, then, the word 'affinity' is one of the most significant words that exists: it is a magic word. For it is the law of affinity which makes it possible for us to draw from the waters of the Cosmic Ocean the best elements, the most radiant and subtle elements with which to build our Body of Glory. I have already talked to you about this Body of Glory, or Body of Light as it is sometimes called, the immortal spark hidden in the innermost being of each man and woman. The Bible mentions it but gives no details. As I have explained in other lectures, we all have a potential Body of Glory within us, but we have to form it by giving it the materials it needs in order to grow, just as a mother nourishes the child in her womb.

How does a mother form her baby? By everything she eats or drinks, by every breath she draws, by every thought she thinks. Simply by living she gives it the materials it needs to grow and develop. It is she who forms her child and she cannot do more than that. She cannot create it. Nor can we create Christ in us: our souls must be impregnated with the divine seed before Christ can be conceived in us. Only then, like a human mother, can we nourish and form Him with everything that emanates from us, with all that is pure and good in our lives.

When, from time to time, we experience a really elevated state of consciousness, when we are moved by the desire to help the entire world, to work only for the Lord, to deny ourselves and do something really lofty and noble, then the particles that emanate from us go to nourish and strengthen our Body of Glory. This is the only way we can make it grow: it can be formed only by the very best in us. If we nourish it over long years with our flesh and blood, with our fluids and our very lives, one day it will become radiant and glowing with light. One day it will become strong, potent and invulnerable to attack. One day it will be immortal, made of immortal, imperishable materials, impervious to wear or corrosion. And when this day comes, our Body of Glory will work wonders within us and around us and Christ himself will be able to use it to accomplish miracles.

Until he has formed this inner body, man remains insignificant, obscure, weak, vulnerable and sickly, and yet every human being carries within him the seed of Christ, waiting to be developed. And this brings us back to the law of affinity. The disciple must surpass himself, rise above himself in order to attract the purest and most luminous particles from the ocean of etheric waters and weld them to his Body of Glory. He can begin immediately, today, to attract a few of these precious particles and, gradually, as the days go by he will attract them in ever greater quantities. In fact, this is what we are doing every morning at sunrise: we are endeavouring to rise to regions above and beyond this earth, to make contact with Heaven, with the sun itself, and to glean some particles of light to incorporate into our Glorious Body. So here, once more, is a fragment from the book of true Science.

For years and years I worked with only one idea in mind: to know and understand the structure of that marvellous edifice, the universe. For years it was my only interest and I spent days and nights out of my body seeking a clear view of that structure and learning how the different elements of the universe all tie in together. I knew that nothing else mattered. The only thing that really matters, that is really essential, is to see the over-all structure, and this is why, as long as man is content to study the disparate elements of the physical world, the world of facts, he will reach only false conclusions. Only by rising to the higher plane of the laws and even higher still to the level of principles, will he reach a vantage point from which he will have the clear view of the whole that I obtained. It took me years, but now I have it, and that is why today I can instruct and enlighten you and give you advice: because my frame of reference is always the cosmic model of perfection.

No one, or hardly anyone, has yet recognized the true value of this philosophy. But this will not always be the case. There are forces at work in the universe which are far more powerful than human beings, and one day these forces will oblige men to appreciate this Teaching at its true value. I am absolutely sure of this and that is why I never worry. I live in the conviction that, sooner or later, everything will fall into place.

For the moment, everything on earth is upside down: anything of real value is scoffed at while things that have no value at all are given first place. See for yourself: people attach enormous importance to gold, jewelry, houses and cars, whereas divine ideas are ridiculed and scorned. This is the exact opposite of the order I have observed in the structure of the cosmos: above all else, in the highest place is an idea, a truth. That is what has pre-eminence in the world above: an idea. Everything else is subservient to that.

Human beings have reversed all the values: nothing is in its rightful place any more. The most vicious and diabolical people are surrounded by wealth and splendour, whereas those who possess the very highest qualities have none of the corresponding exterior trappings. As they are bereft of acquisitiveness they do nothing to obtain worldly riches and so they possess only the strict minimum on the physical plane. Externally, nothing can be seen of all their inner splendour. But this state of affairs will not last forever, because the law of correspondences demands that inner beauty be clothed in outer beauty and that inner ugliness be clothed in outer ugliness. The Intelligence of nature has decreed that it should be so.

In the distant past, when the true order was respected, all those who were inwardly indigent were outwardly poor, too, and those who had great inner wealth also enjoyed visible, outer wealth. Just like the Lord Himself! God, who possesses all qualities and virtues, also possesses the whole universe. It is only here in human society that this order is not respected, but as the law is absolute (that is which is below must become as that which is above), things will be ordained differently one day, and everyone will regain his rightful place : those who are rich in intelligence, kindness and nobleness, will be endowed with corresponding material riches and those who have none of these inner qualities will be poverty-stricken. Obviously it will not be up to human beings to restore the right order, for they have no notion of who is meritorious and who is not. The work will be done by Cosmic Intelligence, for the law of correspondences is an immutable law of the universe.

What I have given you today is a key: use your thoughts and feelings in such a way as to produce emanations and vibrations of a far higher order which, reaching out into cosmic space, will be drawn spontaneously to kindred elements from amongst all the billions that exist. In this way it is within your power to become, once again, masters of your own destiny.

II

The law of correspondences is a physical, chemical, magical and spiritual law which can be expressed in these words: when someone tunes in to what is perfect – be it perfection of intelligence, power, form, colour, perfume or beauty – he benefits from that perfection because he introduces it into his own being. This is an infallible law, and from the first moment that you know it, you can no longer brush aside the idea of perfection without feeling that you are destroying something in yourself. This law is the basis and foundation of all true religion. Why is man told to love God? Because by loving Him and meditating on Him he forms a bond with His perfection and splendour and then that divine splendour begins to take up its abode within him and it is he who grows and blossoms, who becomes beautiful and powerful.

If you fail to respect this law, no one in Heaven or earth can help you. Before you knew

about it, who helped you? The Lord? Certainly
not. He may not even have known what you
were up to! But as soon as you do anything that
touches this law you set in motion a process of
aid and encouragement that eventually frees you
from all your difficulty and suffering. If, in spite
of all your love for God you have not yet
reached this point of freedom, it is because you
built up such a heavy layer of armour around
yourself in previous incarnations that even
though you may now be working in harmony
with this law and, thereby, accumulating tremendous treasures within you, you cannot see or
feel them. But persevere! Little by little your de-
fensive shell will wear away and will end by dis-
appearing altogether. When this day comes, all
that you have stored up through your thoughts,
prayers and contemplation, all that wealth, all
those treasures, all that beauty and splendour,
will pour forth and inundate you. Without realizing it you will have accumulated an ocean of
blessings which is there around you, just waiting
to flood into you!

If your religion is founded only on beliefs or
customs instilled in you by your education or
your environment, it will never be very strong or
durable. True religion is founded on a knowledge of the law of affinity. When you know this

law, then you know that you must love God and think about Him, not because the Church tells you to or because it says so in the Bible, but because there is an absolute law which says that the true beneficiary of that love is yourself and, through you, the whole world. But this knowledge has not yet penetrated into the minds of men : the fact that so many Christians are leaving the Church these days is proof enough of this. Religion as they understood it was not based on anything solid. What they need now is Initiatic Knowledge, the secret knowledge of the Mysteries revealed in the ancient Initiations. A disciple who was guided by his Master through certain initiatic experiences attained a physical perception of reality and could never again doubt what he had learned in this way. His knowledge had become, as it were, part of his own flesh and nothing could ever separate him from it again.

The closer you come to God, the happier you will be and the more you will live in power, omniscience and eternity, because you are drawing to yourself all the particles, forces, rays, currents – call them what you like – which come from Him. Never take counsel from the ignorant, from all those who make pronouncements about the Lord with complete assurance – especially when they declare that He doesn't exist!

What do they think they know that entitles them
to lay down the law so arrogantly? No! The
truth of what I am telling you has been ascer-
tained thousands of years ago and I, myself, have
verified and continue to verify it every moment
of every day.

God has no need of our love, of our gratitude, of our prayers. It is we who need to love
Him and to pray to Him. Some people decide
not to go to Church any more, not to light any
more candles to Him, as a punishment! He has
failed to serve their interests, so He must be punished. Oh! goodness, what weeping and lamen-
tation, how He tears His hair, the poor Lord, all
because He has been dropped by some idiot!
This is the mentality of a lot of human beings. I
repeat, it is to man's interest to believe in God
and to pray to Him. If you refuse God, you must
realize that you will inevitably put other gods in
His place and, as they will have none of His perfection, you will develop their vices, weakness
and illness yourself. Go ahead, turn your back
on Him if you want to. He is so far above us He
will not even notice. He has stopped up His ears
to the chatter of human beings, but they will be
the ones to suffer, because they are depriving
themselves of all His splendours.

Nations and societies which have decided to
get rid of God have, whether they realize it or

not, begun to disintegrate. For the time being they feel perfectly safe, immune from all ill effects, but the day will come when they will begin to prize what they have thrown away. They are like the man who made a pact with the Devil to keep him supplied with money: 'Very well,' said the Devil; 'I'll give you all you need, but on one condition: every time I give you some money you have to give me a hair of your head in exchange.' 'Oh,' said the man; 'That's no problem. Just one hair!' Yes, but in no time at all he was dismayed to find that he was bald, and that led to all kinds of changes in his life. A lot of people say, 'What can you possibly lose by breaking away from God and doing what you really want to do? Nothing's going to happen to you.' Well, that is just where they are wrong. Something does happen: every time you do something wrong you lose a tiny particle of vitality, freshness and charm, and in the end, even if you have gained materially, you will have lost your most precious assets.

I insist, do not let a single day go by without making contact with Heaven for, in this way, thanks to the law of affinity, you will trigger all kinds of processes which will have important repercussions. To my mind the most stupid thing anyone can do is to break off relations with the Heavenly Father. There are all kinds of foolish

mistakes we can make – I hardly need to enu-
merate them to you – but this is the greatest and
most foolish of all, for it opens the way to all the
others. Don't think that I'm asking you to become religious fanatics, to spend your time in
church lighting candles and reciting prayers like
so many poor creatures one sees. Their forbid-
ding expressions are proof enough that, for
them, religion is a question of exterior rites and
practices. If it were really sincere it would have
changed them and there would be some visible
signs of the radiance within. Well, there are
many different ways of understanding religion!

Nowadays religion is not held in as great
esteem as in the past when religion, priests and
the Church were universally respected. Many
priests sense this change of attitude, and try to
keep contact with the masses by organizing all
kinds of popular activities in their churches.
You see them there in the crowd: chubby, rosy-
cheeked and jovial – truly priestly figures, in
churches which have nothing sacred about them
any more, what with the Bingo, folk-music, dis-
cussions and dances that are held there. The
clergy is at a loss to know what to think up next
to attract the crowd, but all their efforts are ir-
relevant. The only thing that can still save the
church from extinction in every part of the

world is Initiatic Science, because it is only in Initiatic Science that a solid basis for religion is to be found.

A great many people never pray any more. They think, 'It doesn't pay! When there's a job or work waiting to be done, what's the point of going off to pray or meditate? It's a waste of time.' Of course, prayer will not afford you any material returns: money, houses, cars, a top-flight job, a rich wife, etc. No, but it has other advantages: when all your thoughts and affections are entirely concentrated on God you are directly in touch with Him and from this communication flow abundant spiritual gifts, strength and light. These advantages are invisible, it's true, but as the invisible side of things is nonetheless real, what you receive has its effect on you and on all those with whom you come in contact. People feel vivified, comforted and consoled, they begin to trust you and to offer you all kinds of advantages, including material advantages. But it all starts with the spiritual side of things.

You should not look for material gains from prayer or from loving God. A lot of people say, 'I pray and pray and where does it get me? I'm still just as poor as ever!' So, evidently they had expected to get rich thanks to their prayers! It is really astounding how distorted an understanding some people have! Humanity needs to learn the truth about the realities and laws of the Invisible World if they are ever going to understand what true science, true religion and true life are all about. For the moment there is a great deal of misunderstanding: they persist in looking for all sorts of advantages and are totally unaware that in the meantime they are receiving nothing but disadvantages.

When you are tuned in to the Lord you attract to yourself His qualities. They seep into you, penetrating your being and making you a radiant, intelligent and well-balanced human being. When this happens, you may even receive material wealth if such is your destiny, but if the first thing you ask for is material wealth, it shows that you still have not understood. To begin with, you will not necessarily have an easy time, but the invisible side of things will soon begin to improve and even if you cannot see this, you can feel it. Do you never have the feeling that a certain person simply by his presence has a calming effect? Some people give you a feeling of peacefulness, you feel that you are a better human being when you are with them, whereas others always seem to arouse the worst in you.

These are intangibles perhaps, you can't see them, but they are no less real for all that.

True religion is based on a knowledge of the law of correspondences. As soon as you plug in to a given source, a power-house or a radio-transmitter, you inevitably start receiving particles from that source. And if you tune in to a different transmitter that sends out messages in direct contradiction to the first, you receive them, too. You cannot see them? No matter, one day you will. Today I am giving you some pearls from the treasure-house of true Knowledge, known in the past only to the great Initiates. If you receive and nurture them you will become invincible.

If someone says, 'I put the Teaching into practice. I do all the things you tell us to do, and look at me! I know I'm unbalanced and neurotic. I'm on the brink of going out of my mind,' I can only reply, 'You're mistaken in thinking that you're putting the Teaching into practice. There must be something inside you to which you are still giving free rein: pride, some disorder in your sexual life or an undisciplined imagination. Or perhaps you're trying to force the pace and achieve great spiritual results much too quickly? None of this is in keeping with the Teaching. It is not the Teaching that is to blame.

It could be that you're not going about it the right way. Look for the cause in yourself.' The Teaching is there precisely to help people to become well-balanced, to make them strong and happy, not to destroy them. So, if things are not all well with you, try to unearth the real cause: the law you have broken or some way in which you have over-indulged yourself and which has led to your present sorry state.

Another person says, 'I don't want anything to do with my family any more. They're not very evolved and not at all mystical. I want to free myself from them completely.' There again I must answer, 'Isn't your reasoning a bit excessive and dangerous? You have bonds that tie you to your family and you can't cut those bonds so easily.' In your reasoning, your decisions, your feelings, if you are too personal, it will always produce some anomaly in you. Therefore, if you suffer from all kinds of ailments and infirmities, look for the cause in yourself and your own behaviour, not in the Teaching.

Let other people believe what they like, but you who are being taught the great laws of life, know that you have an obligation to aim for nobility and perfection. All those who reject religion, thinking that it is more important to work for society no matter whether you believe in

God or not, are on the wrong road because, in the long run, a society without God degenerates. Without a central axis on which to turn, it falls apart, and they themselves will cease to be irreproachable social beings: cupidity, partiality or injustice will inevitably creep in. This is why societies, empires and kingdoms end by disintegrating: they have no stable central point to cling to, to prevent the development of negative forces.

A society that is sound and truly centred on a higher reality, a society that cherishes a sublime, divine ideal, is vibrant with currents so potent that whatever wild beasts still linger within it are rendered harmless: cowed and ineffectual, they no longer dare to make their presence felt, and it becomes much easier to establish just laws and build a society of peace and plenty for all. But when the intensity of the spiritual life is allowed to wane, when the centre or head is absent, then negative forces are once more stirred into activity and take possession of individuals, for there is nothing to keep them at bay. If disasters of such magnitude have engulfed the world in our day it is because human beings have allowed all the divine, beneficial forces within themselves and within society to falter and weaken.

This, therefore, is the life of a disciple: it turns on the axis of a central idea, and that idea

begins by instilling fear and caution into the enemy within. An example on the level of physical
health : people who live very disordered lives
end by ruining their health and begin to be ravaged by tuberculosis, for instance. The doctors
tell them to lead a more regular life : less emotion, excitement and passion, a healthier diet
and adequate sleep. If they follow this treatment,
their bodies secrete certain substances, antibod-
ies which counteract and paralyse the bacilli and
their health improves. Should the patient re-
sume his old way of life, drinking and smoking
and spending his nights in folly, all his defences
crumble, and disease once again gets the upper
hand.

Exactly the same law prevails on the psychological level. The life of the spirit helps us to
build defences against the forces of evil and to
muster our workers and assistants – for there is a
veritable factory in every human being – but if
we become careless and stop living harmoniously, the forces of imbalance and darkness assert
themselves and proliferate, and we begin to de-
teriorate again. Our best bulwark is God Himself, and we must maintain a firm bond with
Him so that the forces which He awakens within
us become strong enough to ward off the evil entities which are always ready to do us harm. If
we want to sever this bond we are perfectly free

to do so but sooner or later that freedom will cost us very dearly.

Now, what I have given you today is a page from true Science, the Science that I have spent my life studying, not in books, certainly, but in my own innermost being. And thanks to this life-long study the secrets of this Science are now crystal-clear to me. And you, too, can reach this certainty: no matter what philosophy happens to be in fashion at the moment and no matter what other people may tell you, never let yourself deviate from this central notion of the Deity. Cling to it, seek it out, keep it always in mind, love it, call upon it. This is the only way to be sure of receiving the potent energies you need to keep you from being harmed by your inner enemies. You may still get bitten from time to time if your defences are not absolutely impenetrable, but little by little you will strengthen them and evil will no longer be able to reach you. Christians sing, 'The Lord is my Shepherd,' but to most of them these are just words, they say them mechanically, knowing nothing of the extraordinary science and magic power hidden in the words.

Believe me, nothing is more important for man than to love his Creator. Nothing is comparable. Because of this love everything falls into place, problems resolve themselves, life becomes

harmonious and, even if we fail to get visible results in this incarnation, it does not matter, for
entities from on high watch over us and when
they see that we are making an intelligent effort,
show their approval by sending us all kinds of
blessings.

6

NATURAL AND MORAL LAW

When you observe the actions of human beings it soon becomes obvious that they are lacking in a sense of moderation both in their options and in their behaviour in general. Either they never stop stuffing themselves with food or they eat too little – and in both cases they undermine their health. Either they work too hard and wear themselves out or they never do a hand's turn and end by becoming completely rusty. And the same is true where sleep, recreation, thoughts and feelings are concerned. Speaking of someone who exaggerates in some way people say that he has 'overstepped the mark', that he has broken certain laws which he should have known and respected.

There are a certain number of physical laws which govern the whole of nature, including our own bodies, and although human beings may not always obey them at least they acknowledge their existence. Unfortunately this is not true when it comes to moral law. Those who acknowledge the existence of moral laws are few and far between nowadays, and even if people still have some faint belief in the necessity for a certain order, most writers, philosophers, artists and scholars expose theories, write books and create works of art whose sole aim is to dispel the last remnants of this belief. But it is precisely the moral laws which I want to talk about today, because when these laws are not recognized, something essential is missing from human knowledge.

The realm of moral law is not divorced from the physical world. You can see that for yourself in the case of a drunkard, for instance. To begin with he is kind and thoughtful, pleasant, cultured, honest and generous – he has all the virtues! But as he begins to drink, these virtues fade away and before long they disappear without a trace. Or take another case: a man has such a passion for gambling that he ends by neglecting his duty and forgetting his wife and children and his job. To begin with, his gambling is an activity with no moral connotations, but in the end, it is the moral dimension of the man that suffers. How is it that humans fail to see the connection between the two worlds? They believe only in the value of the physical, material world. That is all well and good, it is very important. But the moral dimension, the inner, ethical dimension is very closely linked to it.

According to Initiatic Science there are three worlds: the divine world which is the level of ideas, the psychic world which is the level of thoughts and feelings (it is on this level that we find the moral laws) and finally the physical world, the world of forms and materialization. The material world is linked to the moral world which in turn is linked to the far higher world of ideas. If human beings cannot see these connections it is because they have failed to study and observe what surrounds them, and until they do so they will suffer the disastrous effects of their own ignorance.

Ignorance is no defence before the law: even if you do not know the moral laws, if you flout them by your behaviour, you will be obliged to suffer the consequences. When this happens one begins to realize that the moral sphere is also ruled by a certain number of laws and that these laws are far subtler than those which govern the physical world, for they are engraved not only into our physical bodies but also into our souls and spirits. Those who fail to abide by these laws are seen as self-centred egoists by their fellow-men and, before long, they begin to feel deprived of support and friendship. Whatever their offence they will have to pay for it. And what will be the coin of this payment? Well, this can vary considerably: it can be in the form of remorse, pain or suffering, bitterness, regrets and disappointments and sometimes even money. This is something that can be seen on every level.

Everything is connected, related to everything else. The moral domain is governed by immutable, indestructible laws which you should know. They are often ignored because they are not written down anywhere and people think they have the right to do whatever they please. This is not so: until such time as people realize that these laws exist they will never make any real progress. It is unacceptable to go only by your own rules of conduct, saying, 'I'll do what I please!' Why? Because you will pay for it if you do. You think you have every right to do thus and so – all right. Do as you please but know that you will pay for it. In the natural order everything has to be paid for, even happiness and joy, even ecstasy. 'But I haven't any money.' These laws will not ask for your money (only human beings ask for money), but they will ask you to pay with some of your strength, some of your knowledge, health or beauty, some of your inner light. If you manage to analyse yourself you will see that your books do not balance: the bailiffs have been there! That is, Cosmic Forces, the intelligent beings who govern the universe, have visited you and taken away something and you are that much the poorer!

If you want to become very rich you must disobey neither the laws of nature, nor moral laws, nor human laws. Although man-made laws are not of the same kind as the natural laws, as long as one lives in a society in which they still prevail it is preferable to obey them (to respect the Highway Code, for instance). If you break man-made laws without being found out, nature will not hold it against you, it is not her concern. But if you break one of nature's laws, even if society continues to respect and honour you, you will fall ill. Yes, the natural law will put you to bed! Nature will punish you and, go where you will, you cannot escape; wherever you go, the law will catch up with you because your record is filed in your own innermost being.

Nature knew in advance that men would always manage to break her laws so she put miniature tape-recorders into them. And now all she has to do is to glance into us and she can see exactly what we have eaten and drunk, what we have thought, felt or done. Quite impossible to cheat! And you think you can convince me that only human beings make recordings? How could men make anything at all if nature did not give them the idea in the first place? Nature recorded things long before man, but man is too blind to see this. So, nature has taken the necessary precautions, and if man breaks her laws he has to pay.

From now on, therefore, try not to break any laws whether man-made or natural and, especially, try not to break the moral laws which are superior to the natural laws. In point of fact, of course, moral laws are part of nature, for nature includes different degrees or levels. On the lowest level is the purely physical nature. Above that is a more subtle nature which is the level of thoughts and feelings. And the last degree, which is above both of these, is the level of the divine world. Nature too obeys the laws of her highest degree. Just as we have to obey nature's laws, nature obeys the laws of the spirit, for the spirit commands nature. When a man has reached the stage where he can rise above the first two levels, his physical nature and his more subtle nature of thoughts and feelings, he is beyond the reach of laws. He is then so pure, in such perfect harmony with the spirit, he disposes of such tremendous powers that even nature obeys him, and whatever he does he never breaks a law. Only when he has reached this stage can man do exactly as he pleases without there being any danger of his breaking the law.

Only very exceptional beings, those who are predestined to do so, manage to rise above the natural and moral laws. Such beings have always existed, they exist today and they will continue to exist – but they are very rare. They can do whatever they like without ever committing a crime or a sin. I have had some fantastic revelations on this subject but it is very difficult to explain; in fact it is impossible to give you even the faintest idea. It is something which cannot be put into words.

However, I shall try to say something to help you to understand. If a man is very pure and radiates light, whatever he does will always be right. If a man is filthy and full of darkness, if he lives in the nether world, even if he decides to do a good deed, he will always soil whatever he touches. He is like a man whose hands are black with dirt and grease and who tries to wipe a little speck of dust off his friend's face: he only succeeds in making it dirtier. In his desire to purify others, such a man sullies them; in trying to simplify their lives all he does is complicate them. And why is this? Because everything emanating from him is so chaotic and vile that whatever he does is destructive. But if a being is pure light, pure love, pure intelligence, even if he strikes someone, instead of killing the blow saves, because everything in that man and everything that emanates from him is divine. To reach this peak, to dwell in the Sephira Kether, one must have been predestined by the Twenty-four Elders long, long ago in the past. As long as a disciple has still not reached his goal he must accept that he is obliged to respect certain laws.

Human beings readily admit that in their professional work certain types of behaviour are acceptable and others are not, but when it comes to morality, they think there are no rules. This is where they are highly mistaken. When Hermes Trismegistus said, 'That which is below is like to that which is above, and that which is above is like to that which is below', he was proclaiming this fact without going into detail, and his words apply to all levels, all areas, all human activities. A tremendous number of activities, objects, colours, forms, beings and regions are included in these two words 'above' and 'below'.

A lot of people have understood the dictum to mean that what is below, that is, on earth, is similar to what is in Heaven. But this is not true: what is on earth is not like what is in Heaven, the forms and dimensions, the light and the colours, the glory and the splendour are not the same on earth as in Heaven. It is the laws that are the same. Hermes did not specify this because he wanted his words to convey a far vaster meaning, which only those who were capable of entering into the point of view of a great thinker or Initiate would be able to understand.

Thanks to their understanding of the laws which govern the physical world, scientists can boast of amazing achievements, such as the expeditions to the moon, for instance. If they understood the moral laws, their achievements would be greater still, and not only on the material level but also in the vast, infinite realm of the soul and the spirit. They are well versed in physics and chemistry, but there is a spiritual physics, there is a spiritual chemistry they know nothing about. An essential element is missing, therefore, in official science, which is a knowledge of the psychic world governed by moral laws. And since, in addition, today's intellectuals do all they can to erase the last traces of moral sense from human consciences, they are working for the destruction of humanity. Everything will fall apart because of those who deny the existence of moral laws and refuse to abide by them.

It is not always easy to identify these laws, but that is no reason to claim that they do not exist. Nothing can justify you in belittling or denying what I have just said. If you are capable of observation and analysis and if you have enough patience, sooner or later it will become evident to you that every inner transgression of

the law has to be paid for, because our inner
world is governed by the immortal precepts of
eternal law.

You commit a breach of the law and you say,
'I'm still eating and drinking, I sleep well, I'm
still earning money and my health is fine: nothing has changed.' Very well, all that this means
is that you are blind! You cannot see what is
happening on the subtler levels of your being.
You may go on like that for years, trafficking
and conniving without ever noticing that every
time you do something dishonest you lose something. And what is that 'something'? You will
have to find that out for yourselves. What I can
tell you is that I know in advance what you will
lose and what tremendous and fearful changes
will take place in your innermost being. In a few
years you will have lost all your freshness, all
your impetus and, above all, everything in life
will have become utterly tasteless to you. These
are immense losses from the spiritual point of
view, and if you cannot see this it is because you
are still on a level with the animals! It may very
well be that you go on working and making a lot
of money, but you will not be a son or a
daughter of God, supple, alive and radiant with
light. Deep inside you some very big changes
have taken place.

Animals eat, hunt, fight and fondle each other and protect their young; a great many human beings do no more than that. They do not know that they have been sent to this earth with a mission: to manifest the glory of God and to bring to full flowering all that is subtle and divine in their nature. They have been sent to turn the earth into a Garden of Eden. That is their mission, but they have forgotten it. They eat and drink and put down roots in the world and have no desire ever to detach themselves from it. So then they are uprooted and packed off upstairs where they learn that they have wasted their lives and then, obviously, they suffer: Purgatory and Hell are nothing more than that. When they have paid and been cleansed they move up still higher to the first Heaven and then, once again, they come back to earth in order to continue their evolution towards perfection. This is the story of the human race.

Men need to be constantly reminded of their mission on earth, 'What are you here for? Try and remember!' Remember? How can one remember? In an Initiatic School, with the help of the great truths he learns and all the beneficial influences he receives, with the help of the angels, a disciple begins to remember the world of

light he came from and to which one day he will
return. The greatest blessing a disciple can receive is to remember. He will remember all he
has suffered and the faults he has committed as
well as the debts he owes. He needs to know all
this so that he can go and find those he has
wronged in the past, make his peace with them
and atone for his faults, thereby paying off his
Karmic debt. This is what is in store for the disciple – for each one of you. One day you will be
obliged to pay for all that you have taken dis-
honestly from others. I realize, of course, that it
is not much fun to hear all this (especially as
most people prefer to be flattered and to ignore
unpleasant truths about themselves), but even if
you have no desire to learn the truth today, one
day you will have to listen. In fact, you are privileged to be able to learn it here, from me.

Prepare yourselves therefore as I prepare myself, to make reparation for all your mistakes.
Let's suppose that I have been a scoundrel, the
worst kind of firebrand, and that I repent and regret my past ways, and want to atone for my
faults. Let's suppose that I have wronged every
one of you : that I have defiled, robbed and massacred you all. Well, just let's suppose! And
now what? By putting up with you all, loving
and instructing you, I am paying my debt and
making reparation. But what if it were not true

that I had wronged you in the past? What then? Well, so much the better. This is a question I purposely leave unanswered: I have no obligation to tell you why and how I came to earth, nor where I come from. That is my business. But let's presume that I am someone who has broken all the laws and now I am condemned to pay you what I owe you. There! You like to hear me say these things, don't you?

Well, if I can talk about this without embarrassment why should you not decide to reason in the same way and start atoning for your faults towards your husband or wife, your children, your parents, your friends? Of course, I understand. You prefer to believe that you are blameless whereas I am a confirmed criminal. All right, all right. But is it the truth? No matter! If I am capable of admitting in front of you that I am not perfect, you can do so, too, in front of others.

Someone has a son who is always tormenting him and bringing dishonour on him, and he comes and complains to me, 'What have I ever done to God to deserve such a child?' The answer is that you have undoubtedly incurred a debt towards your child in the past, otherwise he would not have been born into your family. Many parents who are just, honest people, have to put up with children who are hooligans. It is really astonishing. In fact it would seem to be impossible according to the laws of nature, they could not have sown such seed, but there is always a reason concealed in the past, for the law is unequivocally just.

Recently a brother came to see me. He was in a great state of anguish because he was unfailingly kind and generous to his family and he received only ingratitude and cruelty in return. The injustice of it was destroying him. So I said to him, 'Would you like me to give you a key, an infallible remedy, the perfect antidote? There is one thing you should know, and when you know it, you will never be angry or in revolt again. On the contrary, you will feel fine. That one thing is this: the Invisible World is using all these difficulties to make you stronger, to free you, to oblige you to think and become a better human being. What is gnawing at you and making you ill is that you think that the way you're being treated is unjust. Think, instead, that it is just and you'll find that you feel much better.' Well he did. He trusted me and began to feel better and is now radiant and in peace. He knows that he is almost certainly paying for past transgressions and that idea has saved him. You have to accept to envisage things this way, otherwise the trials and difficulties will end by destroying your digestive system, your heart or your nervous system.

And today I say the same thing to all of you: if the injustices you suffer torment you, accept the idea that there may be apparent injustice, but in reality it is not so. Even if this were not true, the conviction that it is would help you to free yourself, to suffer much less and to become a better person. I have proved the truth of what I am saying, personally. In the past I did not know about this remedy and I often wondered why certain things happened to me. Now I never need to wonder why, I just think that I am getting my just deserts, even if it is not true. What did Jesus ever do to make him deserve crucifixion? Of course, Jesus' destiny was exceptional. Don't imagine that you are in the same situation! And yet, it can happen that the innocent are imprisoned or put to death. If they rebel against the injustice of it, they simply torture themselves to no purpose. Here on earth, even if you are innocent, it is best to think that you are just as guilty as everyone else for, by thinking this way, you will free yourself.

You have been given the task of discovering within yourselves a spiritual realm governed by immutable laws. The slightest infringement of these laws must be paid for, sooner or later. The thing that puts you off the scent is that payment is delayed. But everything is on record. Every single thing triggers a reaction. You will find this same law in many different areas. Take an example from chemistry: you have to wait quite a long time for a sheet of Litmus paper to turn from red to blue or vice versa. The change comes all of a sudden when just one drop of acid or alkali is added to your mixture. Yes, but that one drop is the last in the whole series. Similarly, if you examine the mechanism of a watch, you will notice that the hands start moving only after several different wheels have begun to move one after another. The time that elapses between the moment when the wheels are first set in motion and the appearance of any visible, tangible result may be long or short, but since the parts are all connected, a result is inevitable.

Suppose that you have a particular vice or passion: you cannot see any immediate repercussions and you continue indulging your passion to excess. This over-indulgence sets invisible wheels moving and they in turn set others and still others in motion until one day, you wonder why you are so ill, so worn out. Your fatigue or your illness started long ago. Today, the bailiff has turned up with the summons! But you should have known that it was bound to happen one day. How is it that human beings have not yet understood this law which prevails everywhere and on all levels? All their tribulations and misfortunes stem from their inability to analyse and interpret the mechanisms of their own physical and psychic organs.

If you really want to become a son of God, a truly complete being living the life of the soul and the spirit, you have to respect the precepts of moral law. There is no other way. The doors are closed to anyone who transgressed these laws. The Invisible World never submits to the capricious whims of disrespectful, anarchical, debauched human beings. 'The Invisible World?' you may ask; 'Did you say invisible?' Yes, exactly! That world is hidden, invisible, and if you tell me that you cannot believe in something you cannot see, I shall have to answer that you have never learned to reason. Are your thoughts visible? And your consciousness, your opinions, your feelings: are they visible? And all your plans for the future: can you see them? No, of course not, yet you are persuaded that they exist. You are ready to fight and even to kill people to defend your convictions which are invisible, too. Have you never realized that your whole life is based on things you cannot see? Only the Invisible World exists with absolute certainty: all the rest is open to doubt. If you deny the reality of the Invisible World, you are sawing off the branch you are sitting on, and one fine day you will find yourself on the ground! The truth of it is that you deny these realities rather than admit that you have never taken the trouble to examine them for yourself and form a valid opinion: you should be ashamed of such intellectual dishonesty. Someone who denies the existence of the Invisible World is signing his own death sentence.

Human beings will continue to suffer until they have understood that the Invisible World is the only reality. I have an argument for ignorant people who cannot admit this. You only believe in what you can see, do you? Very well. Suppose that you live in the lap of luxury and one dark night someone seizes you by the throat and says, 'Your money or your life!' Well, even if you have never believed in life before, because it is invisible, all of a sudden you begin to believe and you're ready to give up all your visible goods for the sake of something invisible. How inconsequential of you! If you were logical you would say, 'Take my life, not my money.' But then, of course, you'd be dead and what good would all your money be to you then? You see, nothing is more precious than what you cannot see. Life is an invisible reality and, in spite of that, you are ready to give up everything else for it. How extraordinary human beings are!

Does the Invisible World really exist? Does it claim our recognition and respect, like the visible world? Yes, it does and far more so. It is high time you became aware of the existence of that subtle level of life and learned to appreciate it. If you do, you will see what happens within you. Even if other people notice no change, inwardly you will begin to live in freedom, joy, buoyancy and inspiration, your life will become musical and harmonious, you will be living true poetry. And if you reach this ideal it will reflect even on your material welfare. People will begin to see the beauty of the life you are living and the whole world will bring you treasures. For everything is connected: inner wealth attracts outer wealth, even if it takes time for the effects to show. If you attain that level of perfection in your inner life, your vibrations and emanations will reach out to the whole world, even to the farthest star, and will bring back to you all kinds of blessings and happiness.

A blessing is already being prepared for you, it is on its way and will soon reach you. When it comes, you may question it, 'Where have you come from, who called you, and when?' 'You did,' will be the answer; 'a long time ago.' Yes, that is how it is. Happiness is on its way, but it takes time to get here for it has to come a long

way. Unfortunately, there are also sorrows on
their way. You may not realize it, but you called
them to you a long, long time ago. Besides, what
else could someone who is lack-lustre, ignorant
and stupid expect? Glory? Dazzling light? A
visit from an Archangel? Impossible! Why? Because he is incapable of attracting such splendour: there is a law of affinity which the Initiates of old concealed in the saying 'Birds of a
feather flock together'. This proverb contains a
vast science, incomprehensible to primitive
men. They could not understand the law of
correspondences (also called the law of affinity,
the law of the echo, the boomerang effect or the
law of polarity) so the Initiates preferred to express it in the form of a popular saying, a piece
of folklore.

'How could I have brought all this misfortune on myself?' you ask. 'By your attitude,
your way of thinking and your behaviour,' reply
the Initiates; 'it was inevitable.' 'And my good
fortune?' 'You have worked hard, made sacri-
fices and been generous.' It is absolutely just.
Heaven does not ask your opinion about what
reward you would like: you are given exactly
and precisely what you deserve.

7

NATURE'S RECORDS

Every living being, everything in creation in fact, has its duplicate, and in the same way everything you do, say, think or feel exists in duplicate. When you do something that affects another, whether it be helpful or harmful, your original action fades and disappears but it leaves its imprint on you in the form of an exact replica. Here again, I am telling you an essential truth that humans are totally unaware of, they never think that what they do for good or for evil has repercussions that reach far beyond the original act. Fortunately or unfortunately, it does not end there : fortunately if what they do is good, and unfortunately for them if what they do is wrong.

Everything that exists in nature therefore, plants, insects, animals, the stars or the mountains, they all have their duplicate or double but for the time being we shall limit ourselves to what concerns human beings. A person's etheric double, which has exactly the same form and functions as his physical body, is sometimes visible to clairvoyants; it can even happen that a man's etheric double becomes separated from his physical body and if this happens he loses his perception of all physical sensations: you can prick, burn or hit him and he will feel nothing as long as the etheric body is separated from his physical body. However, even though it has gone out of the physical body for a time, the etheric double is always in touch with its physical counterpart by means of the Silver Cord. It is only in the event of death induced by illness, a wound, or a severe shock, that the Silver Cord is broken.

But it is not only the physical body which has its counterpart: the astral and mental bodies also have theirs. The double of the astral body provides energy on the level of feelings and the mental double provides energy on the level of thought. If a man's astral double detaches itself, he becomes emotionally numb and indifferent, incapable of feeling or emotion. Similarly, if his mental double detaches itself, he becomes incapable of thinking. These phenomena are still relatively unknown and unexplained. If doctors and psychiatrists were aware of them they would have the explanation of many different kinds of psychological problems which still leave them perplexed. The trouble is that they always look for explanations on the physical level, whereas more often than not they lie elsewhere.

But let us talk about this question of duplicates. You all know that in government or business offices, when an official document, a decree or ordonance, is prepared, there is always a carbon copy or a photocopy: the original is sent to the person or office concerned and the copy is kept on file for future reference. It was not humans who first invented filing systems for their records, but nature itself. Nature keeps a copy of all your actions on file in her archives. And when we move on to the other side and seek admission into Heaven, we take with us the copy —or rather the three copies: physical, astral and mental – which bear the record of all our deeds, thoughts and feelings. The originals have gone who knows where, far away to some other planet or to the stars; you cannot get them back, it is too late. But a certified copy is always on file in your own, inner archives.

When a human being reaches the other world he comes before an assembly of highly evolved spirits who remain with him while he watches the projection of the film of his life on earth. The film is not shown for their benefit: they do not need to be shown his life-story, they know it already. They already know the degree of evolution he has reached, his sins and crimes as well as his good deeds. It is the man himself, poor creature, who needs to see the film, for he is so ignorant he does not know himself. He imagines that he was either a monster or a divinity and as he is apt to be mistaken in either case, he has to be shown exactly what he was.

It is we who need to learn something, not the entities of the Invisible World, and that is why it is we who keep our files within us, so that we can take them with us when we leave this life. Whether you believe this or not will not alter the reality, these are facts and will remain so whatever you choose to believe. Of course, it would be sensible to believe me and to accept the truth, because then you could correct your mistakes and improve yourselves. I am convinced that if everyone knew these vital facts there would be very few who would choose to remain prisoners of their own weaknesses, but as they don't know them they go on living as they have always lived, with no inkling of the consequences of their behaviour. And this is why it is so important to instruct human beings, especially children, and tell them about the laws. Even if they do not really understand what you tell them to begin with, later on they will stop to think about it and, above all, they will have an opportunity to ascertain the truth for themselves.

What happens, for instance, when someone commits a crime? Why is it that he is pursued by a memory which keeps flashing the same picture onto the screen of his mind and never leaves him in peace? The crime is over and done with, a thing of the past. He has nothing to fear since he has left no visible clues behind him. Ah, yes, but the duplicate copy is still with him and he has no idea how to get rid of it. You see, there is no need to go to great pains to study all the sacred books of humanity to find out about these things; the truth is demonstrated every day within each one of us. Why does a man's conscience continue to reproach him with the memory of his crimes to the point that he loses his appetite and cannot sleep at night until he has made reparation? Simply because everything is on record in his innermost being.

Cosmic Intelligence has had plenty of time in which to adjust everything and order the universe with wisdom. It is only in the minds of men that everything is disordered, chaotic and absurd. And no matter what you explain to people about these things their only response is, 'No, no. I don't believe all that.' Who do they think they are? What makes them so sure of themselves? If they are really so superior how is it that in their daily lives they are so puny and weak, so utterly powerless to change the course of events or to extricate themselves from all the problems that besiege them?

So as I have said, everything is recorded. To know this law should be enough to convince you that you should be very careful not to indulge every passing fancy. Every bad thought, even if it only passes through your mind, leaves an imprint on you which will be with you for all eternity, all the more so because once a negative imprint has been made there is a tendency for it to become a pattern, a stereotype, which repeats itself over and over again indefinitely. I have often talked to you about this and explained how you can create new patterns in yourself which will end by replacing the old bad habits acquired in the past. If you do nothing to substitute good patterns for the bad ones, they will stay with you, time and again, in every reincarnation. You must erase them, otherwise there is no reason why they should not reappear each time. Hold on to your good patterns, your qualities and virtues, and work at improving them (there is always room for improvement), but you must also work at correcting your defects.

Human beings often get discouraged because they have no idea how to set about correcting their faults. They spend years struggling against a bad habit, acquired God knows when, and never manage to rid themselves of it. In point of fact, instead of fixing all their attention on a defect, which is the negative result of some destructive act in the past, it would be far better to concentrate on what they can do to build the future. From now on, therefore, say to yourselves, 'Now I'm going to make amends and rebuild,' and each day with unshakeable faith and tenacity and absolute conviction, work to this end. Take all the elements God has given you, your powers of imagination, thought and feeling, and concentrate on projecting the most beautiful entrancing scenes onto the inner screen of your mind. Picture yourself bathed in music and light, picture yourself in the sun surrounded by forms of the utmost perfection, imbued with qualities of kindness and generosity, with a capacity to sustain others and to help and guide them.

Since everything is recorded, you must take care to record only what is purest and best. And once you begin you will see for yourself that you will be so captivated by this activity, so busy and inspired, that it will become an inexhaustible source of joy to you, for you will be building the Temple of God within you. I know of no endeavour more worthwhile than this: to build the Temple of God in one's innermost being, using all the best materials: utterly disinterested thoughts, feelings and acts.

Most human beings are very far from entertaining this ideal. All they are interested in is to record a little interesting information in their brains, without getting down to the real work. The difference between our Teaching and that of all other schools is that in the schools you *learn*, whereas here you *work*. Information can be useful but it does not transform you. Only the work we do ourselves is capable of transforming us, not what we have read or heard. Knowledge can incite us to start working, but we shall never be transformed if we make no move to set certain forces in motion within us. If we fail to act on what we learn we shall always be the same however vast our learning

Of course, it is true that you do learn something here in the Universal White Brotherhood, but the most important thing you receive is the stimulus to start working at your own transformation. You cannot transform your whole being unless you outreach your own limits every day, to find the materials you need. Just like a bricklayer, a mason or a master builder, you have to go out and get your building materials. Some of you will say, 'But I don't get any pleasure out of this work!' and with this remark, of course, they show exactly what class they are in. Every creature in nature falls into a certain class. According to their tastes and tendencies they have found their shelter or their lair, they have chosen their skin, hide, fur or feathers. This is destiny. And one day nature will put us into a certain class, too, according to our preferences and the choices we have made.

In fact, man's destiny is determined by the nature of his needs. For example, if you need alcohol and drugs, if you need to frequent nightclubs every night or to spend your time gambling, your destiny is already traced out for you in advance: moral degradation, financial ruin and possibly prison. And if you need to contemplate divine beauty or to spread peace and light all around you there, too, it is self-evident: you will be rewarded with happiness and fulfilment. How is it that people have never noticed that every need or wish, every desire they harbour, sets them on to corresponding rails which lead automatically either to regions infested with hornets, snakes and wild beasts from which none escape intact or, on the contrary, to regions of brightness and splendour and boundless joy? Man determines his own destination by his own inclinations, tastes and desires.

Some are predestined to be ill, some to meet with failure, others are predestined to be persecuted and victimized, and in each case it is they who have determined or predestined themselves. You may ask, 'Is there no way out, no escape from one's destiny?' and I have to tell you, 'No, there's no escape! Not, at least, during your present incarnation. If you had been wiser and more sensible in your previous incarnation you could have arranged to have far better conditions in this one. The only thing you can do now is to use the vast possibilities open to you to ensure that your next incarnation will be better – and to do this you must work night and day to make new recordings, new patterns, new stereotypes to take the place of your old ones.'

I well know, of course, that what I'm telling you to do is very difficult. How can one find within oneself all the goodwill and energy one needs to undertake and, particularly, to persevere in such a task? But don't forget that although your work begins with yourselves the results you achieve will, in the long run, have a beneficial effect on the whole world. All your other work, all your material activities, however skillfully they may be planned and executed – God knows if they are really any use to other people! All is recorded, filed and computerized and, in the end, when a man dies and goes over to the other side, the heavenly entities he meets do not even ask, 'How have you lived? What have you done? Did you help or comfort anyone, did you guide anyone towards the Eternal Fountainhead?' They never question a human being because they know in advance that he would lie! No, they take a tiny reel of film from him, put it on their projectors and let him see it for himself.

You will think that this is impossible. Not at all! Every one of us has a tiny reel, an atom, lodged at the point of his heart and which contains a recording of every detail of his life. Look at a magnetic recording tape: you have a length of tape and you cannot see or hear anything on it, but put it into the appropriate machine and what do you hear? The Barber of Seville! To make sure you do not start inventing all kinds of stories and trying to justify yourself, you are told to sit down in front of a screen and keep quiet while the film unwinds. And you see everything, absolutely everything you have ever done down to the last detail. History does not relate how your hair stands on end at the sight of it! 'But we haven't got any hair on that point! How can it stand on end?' Well, of course, you have left your physical hair behind, but you have another kind of hair and, I assure you, it does stand on end! And there you are: there is no way of bluffing or lying about your life.

Although it is not explained in quite the same way, all this can be found in the sacred books of humanity and, in particular, in the Egyptian Book of the Dead. In this book it says that when a man dies he comes into the presence of Osiris, his soul is weighed, and so on. There is also the Tibetan Book of the Dead which reveals the different stages of a soul's journey in the after-world, how he is judged and the conditions imposed on his rebirth.

Well, there you have a few words on the law of memory or records. What matters now is to realize how important it is for you to make new and better recordings, better patterns for yourself, every day. What about the old ones? Little by little you will superimpose your new recordings on the old ones and they will be erased. This is a prospect that should encourage you.

Unfortunately, for a long time you will still go on recording a lot of worthless material because you will continue to run in the grooves of your old stereotypes, the old patterns that are so deeply ingrained. But you can at least be aware of what is going on and prevent your situation from getting worse and worse: as soon as you realize that you have recorded something undesirable, react immediately and make amends so as to forestall the evil consequences. Suppose you have entertained destructive thoughts about someone, suppose you have wounded someone with your words or wilfully destroyed something: recognize your fault at once and make immediate reparation. For the moment this will probably be the most you can do, but at least do it! Some people do nothing, absolutely nothing to make amends for a negative thought or act, whereas others at least recognize their fault: 'It slipped out. I couldn't control myself.' This is something that can happen to all of us but we must be aware of it at once and do our best to make amends.

8

REINCARNATION

I

Today I want to talk to you about reincarnation because I realize that some of you are worried about the question and don't know what to make of it. When you were young you were taught that men lived once and once only, and now the idea of reincarnation upsets you: the thing is not clear in your mind.

One could talk endlessly about this subject, describing and discussing the Tibetan, Hindu and Egyptian notions of reincarnation and all their practices and experiments in this area. But what I want to do today is simply to interpret a few passages from the Gospels to prove to you that Jesus himself knew and accepted the fact of reincarnation. You will probably declare that you have read the Gospels through and through and have never come across the word 'reincarnation', and to that I can only answer that there was no reason to mention it explicitly since, in those days, everyone took it for granted. How were the Evangelists to know that one day people would no longer believe? To them, it was tradition, and therefore not essential to their already condensed records. You say you are not convinced? You will be very soon.

Let us see what the Gospels tell us about some of the questions and answers exchanged between Jesus and his disciples. Jesus asked one day, 'Who do men say that I am?' What does this mean? Do you know anyone who asks others to tell him who he is? People know who they are, they don't need to be told by others; for Jesus to have asked such a question means that they believed in reincarnation. And the disciples answer this, saying, 'Some say that thou art John the Baptist, some Elijah, and others Jeremiah or one of the Prophets.' Without reincarnation could Jesus be someone who had long been dead?

On another occasion, Jesus and his disciples encountered a blind man. 'Master,' the disciples asked; 'Who did sin, this man or his parents that he was born blind?' Unless the disciples were referring implicitly to a previous incarnation this question would clearly be absurd. Where and when could the man have sinned otherwise? In his mother's womb? When could he have spent his nights carousing? When did he commit robbery or murder? Either the question implies belief in a previous life or it is meaningless.

Perhaps you will object, 'Yes, but the disciples were simple fishermen. They weren't educated men and they might well have asked some very strange questions.' If that were the case, wouldn't Jesus have reprimanded them? We are told that he did so on many occasions, but in this case he quite simply answers their question: 'Neither he nor his parents sinned...' and this also required an explanation. If the disciples wondered if the man had been born blind because of the sins of his parents, it was because they knew from Jewish law that if a man suffers some infirmity, illness or other affliction it is because he has transgressed the Law, unless – and this often occurs – it is because he is paying for another. When one saw someone suffering, therefore, one could never tell whether his misfortunes were due to his own sins or to the fact that he was sacrificing himself for someone else.

This was the accepted belief among the Jews. The disciples asked the question because they knew that no one would be born blind without good reason, and not, as Christians are told, simply because it pleased God. Jesus replied, 'Neither hath this man sinned, nor his parents, but that the works of God should be made manifest in him.' That is, so that Jesus should heal his blindness, and so that all who saw him do it should believe in him. To the disciples Jesus

said: you have been taught that there are two
reasons why men suffer, either because they
have sinned and are being punished, or they are
free of sin and are paying someone else's debts in
order to hasten their own evolution. But there is
still another category of people: those who have
finished their evolution and are not obliged to
return to earth again, who are free, but who nev-
ertheless do return, accepting to endure suffering, disease or infirmity, even martyrdom, in
order to help mankind. The blind man belongs
in this category: 'Neither hath this man sinned
nor his parents, but that the works of God
should be made manifest in him.' This blind
man was a saviour for countless others.

If you are still unconvinced, let me give you
more evidence. One day Jesus was told that John
the Baptist had been thrown into prison. The
text says simply, 'Now when Jesus heard that
John had been put in prison, he departed to Gal-
ilee.' Some time later John was beheaded by
order of Herod. After the Transfiguration the
disciples asked Jesus, 'Why then do the scribes
say that Elijah must come first?' Jesus answered,
'Elijah truly is coming first and will restore all
things. But I say to you that Elijah has come already, and they did not know him but did to him
whatever they wished. Likewise the Son of Man
is also about to suffer at their hands.' And the

Gospel adds, 'Then the disciples understood that he spoke to them of John the Baptist.' Clearly, therefore, Jesus was saying that John the Baptist was the reincarnation of the Prophet Elijah. Furthermore, it says in the Gospels that when the angel appeared to Zacharias, the father of John, to tell him that his wife Elizabeth would bear him a son, the angel added, 'He will also go before Him in the spirit and power of Elijah.'

Now let's see what the Prophet Elijah had done to deserve being beheaded when he returned to earth as John the Baptist. It is an interesting story. Elijah lived at the time of King Ahab whose Queen Jezebel was the daughter of the King of Sidon. Because of Jezebel, Ahab and all his people believed in Baal and worshipped that god. Elijah was sent by God to reproach Ahab for being unfaithful to the God of Israel, and told him, 'As the Lord God of Israel lives, before whom I stand, there shall not be dew nor rain these years, except at my word.'

Elijah then went and hid in the mountains, as God ordered him, to avoid capture. At the end of three years the country was ravaged by drought and famine and the people were starving. Again God sent Elijah to King Ahab. When Ahab saw him he cursed him bitterly for causing the drought. But Elijah answered, 'I have not troubled Israel, but you and your father's house

have, in that you have forsaken the command-
ments of the Lord, and you have followed the
Baals. Now therefore, send and gather all Israel
to me on Mount Carmel, the four hundred and
fifty prophets of Baal... who eat at Jezebel's table.' When they were all assembled, Elijah told
them they would now see who was the true God.
'I alone am left a prophet of the Lord; but Baal's
prophets are four hundred and fifty men. Therefore let them give us two bulls; and let them
choose one bull for themselves, cut it in pieces,
and lay it on the wood, but put no fire under it;
and I will prepare the other bull, and lay it on
the wood, but put no fire under it. Then you call
on the name of your gods, and I will call on the
name of the Lord; and the God who answers by
fire, He is God.'

The prophets did as he said and all morning
long they invoked the name of Baal, 'O Baal,
hear us!' There was no answer, and Elijah
mocked them, saying: 'Cry aloud, for he is a
god; either he is meditating, or he is busy, or he
is on a journey, or perhaps he is sleeping and
must be awakened.' The prophets cried all the
louder, and because they had some knowledge of
magic, they slashed their bodies, hoping that the
blood would attract evil spirits and elementals to
set fire to the altar. But nothing happened and
Elijah decided that was enough. Then, taking

twelve stones 'he built an altar in the name of the Lord; and he made a trench around the altar... and he put the wood in order, cut the bull in pieces, and laid it on the wood and said, "Fill four waterpots with water, and pour it on the burnt sacrifice and on the wood."' After they had done this three times and the trench around the altar was full of water, 'Elijah the prophet came near and said, "Lord God of Abraham, Isaac, and Israel, let it be known this day that You are God in Israel, and that I am Your servant, and that I have done all these things at Your word. Hear me, O Lord, hear me, that this people may know that You are the Lord God..."'

Then the fire of the Lord fell from Heaven with such power that everything was consumed, nothing was left, neither victim, nor wood, nor stones, nor water. The terrified people fell on their faces in recognition of the true God, the God of Elijah. Wherupon Elijah, somewhat overzealous after his victory, led the four hundred and fifty prophets to a mountain stream and slit their throats.

From this tale you can see that it was only to be expected that Elijah would have to submit to the same treatment and be beheaded: that is the law. When Jesus rebuked Peter for cutting off the ear of Caiphas' servant in the Garden of Gethsemane he was referring to this selfsame law: 'Put your sword in its place, for all who take the sword will perish by the sword.' However, the truth of this law is not always manifested during the same incarnation. We know how Elijah died: not only was he not beheaded but he was caught up and carried straight to Heaven in a chariot of fire! It was only later on, when he returned as John the Baptist, that he had to pay the price. Jesus knew who John had been and the destiny he had to fulfil and although he spoke such magnificent words of him: 'Among those born of women there is not a greater prophet than John the Baptist', yet he made no attempt to save him. He did nothing because he knew that justice must take its course. Now you see why Jesus left the country: he was not meant to save John the Baptist. The law is the law.

Now let us go still further. I will show you that nothing makes sense without reincarnation: nothing in life, nothing in religion. Ask a priest or pastor who decides that one person should be rich, handsome, intelligent, strong and successful in everything he undertakes, and another one sickly, ugly, poor and miserable and stupid: he will answer that it is the Will of God. He may add all kinds of explanations about grace and predestination but that doesn't make it any clearer. It all boils down to one thing: the Will of God. But if you analyse it – and since God has given us our minds why should we let them go rusty from disuse? – this simply means that God is capricious, that He has arbitrary whims and wishes and that He gives great wealth to some and nothing at all to others. Very well! I can accept that: after all He is God and His Will is always magnificent. I can only bow before it. But what I find incomprehensible is that He should be offended and fly into a rage when people to whom He has never given anything good, do something silly or stop believing in Him and turn to crime. If He has given them that mentality, if it is His Will that they should have so little intelligence and feeling, why does He then have to punish them for it?

God is almighty and omniscient: couldn't He create all men good, honest, intelligent, wise and devout? Couldn't He make all men splendid? Not only is it His fault if people commit crimes but He then has to punish them for doing so! No, no! I cannot go along with this. I agree that God is all-powerful, I agree that He should do as He sees fit, He is irreproachable, but then why is He not also consistent, logical, and just? The least He could do is leave humans alone; but no, He sends them to Hell for all eternity. That astounds me. For how many years did they sin, thirty, or forty? Well, let them remain in Hell for forty years: no more. But for all eternity? No, I can't go along with that. Just think about it. Use your reason. Ah, but people don't reason; they don't dare to think; their minds are paralysed by what they have been taught. They behave as though it were a crime to think for oneself, but then what are our minds for? If God gave us intelligence surely He wants us to use it!

From the moment we accept the notion of reincarnation all that is changed. God really is Master of the Universe, all powerful, all noble and all just, and it is our own fault if we didn't know enough to use all that God gave us from the very beginning and had to make our own costly experiments. As God is also most generous and most tolerant, He lets us do as we wish, He says to Himself, 'Well, they will suffer and run into trouble, but it doesn't matter, I will always have plenty of love and plenty of everything to give them when they are ready for it. They have enough reincarnations ahead in which to learn!' He leaves us free and whatever happens to us is our fault. Why does the Church put all the blame on God? You answer, 'The Church doesn't blame God, it simply abolished the idea of reincarnation.' It comes to the same thing, if you think about it.

The Christians believed in reincarnation until the fourth century, as did the Jews, Egyptians, Indians, Tibetans, etc. But no doubt the Church

Fathers said to themselves that this belief gave people too much time, they were improving too slowly, and if the idea of reincarnation was eliminated they would make more rapid progress for they would think that they had only one life in which to become perfect! Gradually the Church invented more and more horrors in order to frighten people into obedience, so that by the Middle Ages all they believed in was devils, Hell and everlasting damnation! Belief in reincarnation was abolished so that fear and dread would force people to live better lives, but the result was that not only did they not improve, they became worse and worse – and ignorant to boot! We must get back to this belief. Without it nothing is true, nothing in life makes sense, God is a monster of cruelty.

The question of reincarnation has been dealt with seriously and scientifically and I don't intend to discuss it further. There are enough books about every aspect including the way in which the Lamas of Tibet choose a new Dalai-lama. I'll just tell you of one really extraordinary case I met with whilst I was still living in Bulgaria. One day a husband and wife came to the Brotherhood; they were worried about their little boy who was always saying things that seemed incomprehensible to them. 'One day we

went for a walk with him,' they told us; 'And
although he had never been that way before,
when we got to a certain place he said at once
that he knew it well and had often been there.'
Now this couple had had another son who had
accompanied them to this place, but that first
son was dead and no one had ever told this other
little boy about him. But the child went on,
'Don't you remember? This is where I hid when
I didn't want to go to school... and there is the
river where I drowned!' And it was all true:
their first son had drowned in exactly that spot
but this little boy had never heard of it. It was a
clear case of the first child coming back to reincarnate in the same family. Such a case is very
rare but it has been known to happen. Some
children remember their past life up to the age of
seven, but their mothers instead of listening, are
apt to slap them and tell them to stop talking
nonsense. After one, two, three attempts, the
child gives up and doesn't talk about such things
any more.

Now as we have seen, although the word
reincarnation does not appear in the Gospels, it
was common belief at that time, part of the tradition. Here is another example. Jesus said, 'Be
ye perfect as your Father in Heaven is perfect.'
What are we to think? Either Jesus was being

unreasonable in asking common sinners to attain the perfection of their Heavenly Father in the space of a few years, or he didn't realize Who his Heavenly Father was; in either case, it doesn't say much for his own intelligence! Actually, he was talking about reincarnation. Jesus certainly didn't believe that anyone could become perfect in one lifetime, but he knew that if you long for perfection and work toward it during one incarnation after another, you will eventually reach it.

What does Moses say in the Book of Genesis when describing the Creation? 'And God said, Let us make man in our image, after our likeness: and let him have dominion over the fish of the sea and over the fowl of the air and over cattle... God created man in His image, in the image of God created He him.' What happened to the word 'likeness'? God doubtless intended to create man in His image and in His likeness, that is, perfect like Him; but He did not, He created him in His image only. He gave man the same faculties as Himself, but not the fullness of those faculties, that is, the resemblance. An acorn is the image of its father, the oak tree, it has all the same possibilities, but it hasn't the likeness, it does not resemble the oak tree until it has been planted and grown to maturity. Man is the image of God, he has been given the same wisdom, love and power, but in such infinitesimal degrees compared with the Wisdom, Love, and Power of God! In time, when man develops, he will resemble God, and he will possess all of God's virtues in abundance. Do you see now how this progress, this passage from image to resemblance cannot take place without reincarnation? God said, 'Let us make man in our image and after our likeness,' but He didn't do it. 'God created man in His own image, in the image of God created He him.' Moses revealed the idea of reincarnation in the omission of the word likeness and the repetition of the word image.

But people don't know how to read what is written in books, still less what is written in the living Book of Nature which is full of references to reincarnation. Take the example of a tree: only the Cabbalists have really understood the meaning of a tree, and the great cabbalistic symbol, the Tree of Life, is an image of the universe in the form of a tree in which every living creature has its place, either in the roots or the trunk or as leaves, flowers or fruit. This vast and comprehensive science says that all existence, all activity, all regions, have a place on the Tree of Life. At different times of the year, the leaves, flowers and fruit fall to the ground where they decay and become fertilizer for the roots. It is the same for human beings: when a man dies he is reabsorbed into the life cycle of the Cosmic Tree, only to reappear in the form of a branch, leaf or flower. Nothing is ever lost, beings appear, disappear, and reappear ceaselessly on the wonderful tree that is the Tree of Life.

So you see, reincarnation is written on everything, everywhere in life. Where else can we see it? In the phenomenon of evaporation, for instance. Water evaporates out of the ocean into the air, where it turns to snow or rain, and then falls back into the ocean. A drop of water doesn't disappear, it travels all over the world, rising high into the sky and falling back down on mountains and valleys, sinking deep down into subterranean stratas, changing colour as it goes, from yellow to red to green. This phenomenon of water rising and falling vividly illustrates the law of reincarnation: a spirit is like a drop of water, constantly learning as it journeys through space and time until it reaches perfection.

Do you want yet another argument? Very well, take this one: before going to bed at night you undress. One by one, off comes your jacket, sweater, shirt and socks, etc. Night-time and sleep symbolize death, and the clothes you take off represent the different bodies you shed after death: first the physical body, a week or two later the etheric body, and a good deal later the astral body. It takes much longer to shed one's astral body because it is the seat of our passions and desires. The astral and the lower mental planes are the region we call Hell, where we must remain until we are purified. Not until we are free of the mental body can we enter Paradise, the first heaven, the second heaven and the third heaven : seven heavens in all according to tradition. Only when we are stripped of everything and are completely naked, that is purified and free of all impediments, do we enter the seventh heaven of Paradise.

Then, once again morning comes, symbolizing another birth, another incarnation. Once again you put on your clothing, your shirt, sweater, jacket, etc... When a child is to be born, he must clothe himself in each one of his divine bodies, then the mental body, the astral and etheric bodies and, finally, the physical body. You see, every night of your life, you have undressed and every morning you have dressed, without realizing that you were imitating the motions of incarnation and disincarnation. If we could interpret our little daily habits, our behaviour and work, what it means to eat, to breathe and so on, we would make many discoveries. All the great mysteries of the universe are reflected in our acts, in our speech and gestures but you have to study in an Initiatic school to learn how to decipher them.

Some people are waiting for the Church to pronounce its official recognition of reincarnation before making up their minds – but this may not happen for a long time yet! I have often had occasion to talk with members of the clergy and I have seen that, although they dare not admit it openly, many of them do believe in reincarnation. If you don't accept the fact of reincarnation you will never fully understand your present situation nor the events of your life (why you are persecuted and dogged by misfortune or, on the contrary, why you always find help and encouragement on your way), and you will never know what you should be doing to prepare for your next life. When you don't have the truth to guide you how far can you go?

Belief in reincarnation is one of the corner stones of morality. So long as human beings are unaware of the existence of the law of cause and effect which is operative from one incarnation to the next, no amount of preaching or sermonizing will ever do much good. How many people do you know who still believe that they will burn in Hell for all eternity because of their sins? Of course, there are people who don't believe in reincarnation and who show themselves to be naturally honest and good. The only trouble is that one can never be sure how long it will last: an unexpected turn of events can arouse primitive instincts such as fear, lust, vengefulness and so on, which can overpower them and, all of a sudden, they are no longer so honest or so good! Yes, this can happen simply because their morality was not built on a firm foundation: knowledge of the Law.

As soon as you acknowledge the law of reincarnation you begin to understand that every event of your life (birth, marriage, personal encounters, accidents, successes and so on) is significant, for everything stems from a specific cause whether it be recent or of long standing. This understanding influences your feelings and reactions to events because once you realize that everything has its meaning you are no longer tempted to rebel or to try and solve your problems with hatred and violence. When you recognize that, whatever hardships you may have to put up with, they are the direct result of your own past faults, you accept the fact and cease trying to blame others for your misfortunes.

And finally, belief in reincarnation is a stimulus to developing your willpower: you become strong and steadfast, you avoid doing anything reprehensible that would entail more suffering in the future and you persevere in the work of building a future full of light.

Once you know and acknowledge this law of reincarnation the light is yours and your powers of comprehension are greatly enhanced. Warmth is yours: you can be happy and rejoice in the thought that sooner or later you will attain your goal of perfection. And life is yours: you become active and full of initiative in the creation of your own future. Aren't these three enormous advantages? And they all flow from a belief in reincarnation!

II

When we read the lives of Saints, Prophets or
Initiates and see how they suffered we feel almost indignant: 'Why did they have to go
through such martyrdom?' we might wonder,
'They hadn't done anything to deserve it.' But
that is where we would be wrong. The reason
must be sought in their past lives, for even when
we re-establish the divine order within ourselves, it doesn't mean that we have paid our
debts, or that our past life is erased. We have to
pay to the last penny before we can be entirely
free.

Take the case of the disciples: they were with
Jesus constantly, they lived in the Light and followed the divine Teaching, they harmed no one,
what had they done to deserve being thrown to
wild beasts or massacred? And why did Jesus do
nothing to help them? He did nothing because
he knew they had not finished paying their
debts. They had no doubt committed some

faults in previous incarnations for which they had been unable to make reparation before leaving the world. The Scriptures tell us, 'Do not let the sun go down on your wrath', and 'Before the sun sets, go and forgive your brother.' But this advice has never been fully understood: if we take it literally it doesn't give us much time to patch things up with our brother, does it? Especially in winter when the sun sets early! But the sun in this instance is not the physical sun in the sky: 'sunset' in the symbolic language of the Initiates, means the end of our present life on earth, the moment when man leaves this world for the next. So, in actual fact, he is given plenty of time. But once his time has run out, if he has forgotten to pay or if he hasn't known that he must settle his debts before the sun sets, then the law of Karma goes into effect. Everything we do is noted, everything leaves an imprint that hardens and crystallizes, there is no getting round it. Every last penny has to be paid whether before the sun goes down for you or at some time in the future.

And you who follow a spiritual Teaching and live in the Light, you too are subject to mishaps and misfortune. The fact that you are in an Initiatic school does not necessarily mean that you are immune to all negative influences. The only way you can be sure that no harm can touch you is to be free of all past debts. If you still owe something, then Teaching or no Teaching, Light or no Light, you are going to have to pay. Perhaps, now, the question is a little clearer: you are faithfully following this Teaching, you are living in the Light, everything you do is right and good – but you have to remember one thing: the good in your life will bear fruit in the future, not in the immediate present. So when you have problems, therefore, you must accept them and say, 'Lord God, I know that none of this can destroy whatever good I have done. So much the better if I have to suffer now because that means that I'm being given the chance to pay off my debts. Now that I understand why these things happen I have no intention of rebelling against my lot; I don't ask to be spared.'

Perhaps you will say, 'Even Jesus was crucified: does that mean that he had a Karmic debt to pay?' No, in the case of Jesus it was a totally different matter. We are touching, here, on the vital question of sacrifice. There are beings who agree to sacrifice their lives and accept terrible pain and hardship even though they owe nothing. But such beings are the exception. When one does not understand this whole question of reincarnation in detail one is liable to be very much mistaken in one's judgments.

People can be put into four different categories insofar as the law of reincarnation is concerned. The first category consists of those who are so ignorant and unaware, so lacking in all inner light or moral sense that they live a life of crime. They break every law, therefore, and run up a very big debt, and when they reincarnate they find themselves obliged to put up with terrible conditions in order to pay their debts and make reparation. Their lives are not happy.

In the second group are more evolved beings who try to develop the qualities and virtues that will lead to their freedom. Even so, it isn't possible to settle all one's debts in one incarnation; they must come back again to complete their task. This time they will be given better conditions, they will be allowed to be useful on a higher plane, but they must still keep coming back until their debts are all settled and they are free.

In the third group are those who have reached an even higher degree of evolution and who return to earth in order to carry out certain specific tasks. They have very few debts to pay and are given a great deal of time in which to work on the level of their higher consciousness for good. Once they leave the earth their mission is accomplished and they never come back.

Some of them, however, are willing to give up that happy state of bliss and boundless freedom which is theirs in the intimacy of God. They are so filled with pity and compassion for suffering humanity that they leave this sublime state of their own accord and return to earth to help mankind, even though they know that it may mean torture and a cruel death. Others, who wish to continue a spiritual task begun on earth may, without actually incarnating, enter into the body of another highly evolved being on earth, and work through him. Jesus referred to such a possibility when he said, 'If anyone loves me, he will keep my word; and my Father will love him, and we will come to him and make our home with him.' Such beings are not obliged to reincarnate, therefore. Without having to assume a physical body of their own they can enter into a living man and accompany him every step of the way, from the womb to childhood, youth and maturity, working with, in and through him.

Many people would like to be free but they have a mistaken idea of what it really means. They do everything possible to avoid their obligations, shirk their duty and sever the ties that bind them to others – and then they think they have won through to freedom! But that is no

way to be free. The first step towards true freedom is to pay one's debts : all one's debts! People want to free themselves from their wives,
their children, their employers. Many even commit suicide because they want to be free of society and life itself. But you must get this into
your heads : you will never know freedom until
you have paid all your debts and wiped out your
Karma.

It is right and normal to want to be free but
your freedom must be achieved in conformity
with divine law, and there are very few who
know how to do this. Even here, in the Brotherhood, many of you still put the problem the
wrong way round : you want to become indepen-
dent by escaping from your obligations. It is as
though you had been to a restaurant and eaten
to your heart's content and then tried to slip out
without paying the bill! It's dishonest and dis-
honourable, and the spirits of light above us will
never countenance this attitude. People imagine
that they have freed themselves because they
have abandoned their old job – or their old wife!
But if you do this you will simply be jumping
from the frying pan into the fire : all kinds of
other problems will be lying in wait for you to
prove to you that you are on the wrong track.

The best way to liberate oneself is to be loving, and the worst way is to go on being selfish,

crafty, calculating and stingy. Every time you show generosity and kindness, every time you give, every time you sacrifice yourself, you work toward your liberation. This is why, instead of clinging to possessions, instead of always trying to dodge the issue, instead of always calculating the advantages you can get out of every situation, you must learn to give, give, give! Just look at how people behave when they are in the process of getting a divorce or a separation: how desperately they defend their own interests! Well, what they don't realize is that because of this attitude they will be obliged to meet and come to terms with each other again in future incarnations.

It is love, kindness, mercy and generosity that set a disciple on the path of true liberation. Of course, I know that if you say that to the average human being he will take you for an imbecile, because the average human being is not guided by this light; he doesn't know the true value of generosity. But an Initiate knows how important it is to give, to help others, to be generous and magnanimous; he knows that this is the best way to free oneself. So give! Give always more than is demanded by justice alone, for by doing so you will free yourselves all the sooner.

III

It happens with nations, countries and peoples as it happens with human beings and all living creatures: they are born, they grow and mature, and when they are old they have to give way and make room for others. Everything that lives follows the same curve, giving what they have to give and then dying away as though to rest, before springing up again with renewed gifts to be distributed. We have seen this pattern repeated time and time again by civilizations and even by religions: a religion arises, little by little the scope of its influence grows and strengthens until it reaches a peak and decline sets in: the initial impetus wanes, it becomes rigid and barren and loses its mastery of the keys to life. Even the Mystery Religions, event the great Temples of Ancient Egypt, guardians of the Keys, of Knowledge and of the Powers have trodden this path. What is left of them today? Where are all those hierophants? Where is all that lost

Science? They have come and gone according to the unchanging laws of life : every living creature that is born must also die and make way for others. Only that which has no beginning will have no end.

Look at Ancient Greece, at the numbers and the exceptional creative genius of its poets, playwrights, painters, sculptors, architects and philosophers. And look at Greece today! A country is like a river : the river bed never changes but the water flowing in it is always fresh, always changing. The inhabitants of the river are the countless drops of water that come and go, moving on towards the sea, while millions of other drops take their place. When they reach the sea and are warmed by the sun, they become light and subtle enough to rise into the atmosphere until it is time for them to come back in the form of rain or snow, to join the torrents and rivers and, once more, to go coursing down the mountains and through the valleys. It is the never-ending cycle of death and new beginnings.

A country, then, is a river and its citizens are always new and different and come from many different horizons. Or, if you prefer, a country is like a house which is destined to be occupied by successive groups of people. For years the house is filled with a joyous atmosphere of music, song and harmony and then, with a change of tenants, the atmosphere also changes and becomes more prosaic or more turbulent. It is still the same house but the climate is quite different. The destiny of a country can be explained in the same way : Greece is still the same country geographically, but the inhabitants are not the same as those who lived there three thousand years ago or more. And this holds true for all countries.

Perhaps you will ask, 'How is it that some people, the Tibetans for instance, seem to be able to hold on to the same concepts, traditions and customs for thousands of years?' Comparison with the human organism will perhaps give us the answer : the cells of a human organism are constantly changing and being renewed. From one day to the next they are never the same but they continue to do the same work. Or, if you like, compare it with a factory : the personnel is constantly changing, workers are dismissed or retire and new ones are hired to replace them. A new worker is trained in advance and knows what is expected of him. Similarly, entities who reincarnate in Tibet are already trained in Tibetan ways ; they have an affinity for Tibetans, and are prepared to live there. And Tibetans who are prepared to be like the French, reincarnate in France ; there are many former Tibetans in France, even here in the Brotherhood.

You may ask, 'What about the Jews that have been persecuted for so many centuries?' The Jews who were persecuted and martyred were entites from many different countries who reincarnated into Jewish families because it was their Karma to be persecuted or massacred, but they had not necessarily always been Jews. Heaven arranged for them to be born into a Jewish family at a certain time so that they could pay their debts. And the same thing happened in Greece: entities came from elsewhere to reincarnate there, perhaps from Bulgaria, because the two countries have always hated each other and people often reincarnate amongst their former enemies. Many Greeks have reincarnated in Bulgaria, whether as reward or punishment I don't know!

When you hate someone the effect is the same as if you loved him: you create a bond between you. Hatred forges bonds just as powerful as those of love. If you want to be free of someone, if you wish never to see him again, don't hate or love him. Just be indifferent to him. If you hate him you will be binding yourself to him with a bond that no one will ever be able to undo; you will constantly have to associate with him for centuries to come. Yes indeed! You did not realize this, did you? People imagine that hatred cuts them off from those they hate: on the contrary, hatred is a force that binds you to those you hate just as love binds you to those you love. The nature of the bond is not the same, of course: love produces certain effects and hatred others, but the effects of hatred are just as powerful and just as inevitable as those of love. If the nations of the world knew this they would surely realize how ridiculous and also how dangerous it is to hate others.

You must not be surprised or offended if I tell you that France will soon lose her remaining men of genius. The world has received great treasures in the past from French artists, writers and philosophers, but if the country continues to turn away from Heaven, the source of all this wealth, then future men of genius will choose to incarnate in other countries. Truly great minds are universal in spirit; they have no special attachment to one country. They are citizens of the world. Countries may argue and quarrel over them but if you ask them what they think about it they will tell you, 'We feel at home anywhere in the world. Our homeland? The universe!' Besides, when you get to the next world the question of nationality means nothing. Can't you just picture all those French and German soldiers who died in the two World Wars, meeting on the other side and toasting each other, laughing at how stupid they had been to kill each other when they were all sons of the same Eternal Father?

It is no problem at all for the Entities of the Invisible World to let one country slide into decadence while they raise another to great glory. Just why they do this is their secret. Look at Bulgaria for instance: a few centuries ago, it was a miserable downtrodden country that never produced anything in the way of thinkers or artists or scientists, and now all that is beginning to change, everything is improving. Neither the glory of a country nor its decadence last forever. And what about China? How many centuries has it taken China to stir itself from sleep and shake off its lethargy? Now that it is beginning to rouse itself the rest of the world looks on in fear and trembling! How do you explain that? Who decides these things and why?

It is the Heavenly Hierarchies above who make these decisions. For them it is easy, like giving aid to underdeveloped countries: if a country is poor and backward one of the richer, more advanced countries sends in teams of economists and technicians of all kinds and within a few years the country is on its feet. The Invisible World does the same: It dispatches an elite team of engineers and scientists, specially chosen souls, with the mission to renew the culture and civilization of a country. Sometimes all it takes to set a country right very rapidly is just one really good political leader.

I am sorry if it distresses you to be told that your country is losing its grip, but it is not my fault! All I can do is recognize what is happening and state the facts. I have no nationalistic feelings; I'm neither Bulgarian nor French I'm a citizen of the universe. I belong to the Sun, not to the Earth, so why should I quarrel about any one country – Greece, France or Bulgaria? National boundaries mean nothing to me. There is one thing I have noticed though, and that is that scientists in the Slavic countries have gone further than any others in the field of parapsychic research: telepathy, psychometry, clairvoyance, divining and so on. In spite of the fact that the signs are not visible yet, the day is approaching when Russia will abandon Marxism, and the Communists will be our brothers in the great Universal White Brotherhood.

And yet, although these parapsychic discoveries in Russia are already a great step forward, they amount to barely one-hundredth of what I have revealed to you over the years. One day, though, Initiatic Science will be known throughout the length and breadth of the world. Not, of course, the very highest degrees of this Science :

there will always be certain limits, certain secrets to which human beings may not have ac-
cess, for they are not yet fit to be entrusted with
the ultimate Truth. By nature they are too in-
clined to use their discoveries for their own profit and in order to conquer and dominate others.
But certain important truths will be brought to
light and known throughout the world, and then
it will be the dawn of the new Solar civilization.

IV

'The least little flower that makes its appearance on earth is linked to the whole universe and needs the consent of all of Nature to survive. If it appears before its time Nature can withhold her support and the flower will die.

'And for each one of you, too, the whole of Creation had to consent to your appearance on earth. Perhaps you will think that because you are somebody quite unimportant it is unlikely that Nature should have been in any way concerned with your birth; and yet it is so. Every detail, including the amount of food and drink you will consume during your lifetime, is noted down somewhere, and for you to appear when you did, the Cosmic budget must have had room for you at that time. Everything is connected to everything else, every living thing is part of the Cosmos, and nothing can appear in Heaven or earth without the consent of all Creation...'

I know this idea will surprise and perhaps shock some of you, for it is not the usual way of looking at things. People believe everything happens by chance, that nothing is intentional or planned in advance, that there is no higher Intelligence to guide the phenomena of life on earth, and it is this mistaken philosophy which prevents them from understanding what goes on in the world.

Take a tree, for instance. All of Nature must agree to participate in its development before the tree can grow and bear fruit, it cannot exist unless the elements it needs are supplied by the earth, water, air, sun and heat, and sometimes human care. A tree needs the help of all Creation, but as this action is imperceptible, the tree is thought to be there simply by chance. A man also exists, breathes and moves because he has the help of all Creation. If a single element is withheld, if he is denied air, or water, or vitamins and hormones he dies. Where do these vital elements come from? From the Universe, in its willingness to participate.

When a human being is to be born into the world, do you think it simply happens like that —just by chance? Is that how businesses, families and governments are run? By chance? 'Well, no. Of course not,' you'll say; 'But in human organizations there are special people whose job is to calculate expenses and establish the budget, to plan how much to spend on food, heating and upkeep, where to cut down, how many workers can be dispensed with and how many new people to hire, and so on.' Well, doesn't it seem reasonable, then, that human beings arrive on earth in response to a plan which has been approved by someone? What makes you think that although men plan and organize resources on the national, urban and family levels, there is no equivalent foresight or planning by Nature for every new human being who arrives on earth? Human ignorance is indeed abysmal!

The fact is that there exists an extraordinarily well-planned, well-balanced economy in the universe which determines the number of human beings that shall be born, when they shall be born and how long they shall remain on earth. Every human need is provided for in advance and yet people still imagine that it all happens haphazardly that, even for someone like Jesus, no one decided exactly when he should come, no one consulted the astrological aspects to determine the most auspicious moment. Jesus, they think, just 'happened', nobody quite knows why! No! The truth is that the most exalted Beings planned the exact moment of his coming. Nothing is ever left to chance. Even the advent of Hitler was planned in ad-

vance so that many people – including himself –
should learn a hard lesson.

Perhaps you are wondering how the Invisible
World can possibly foresee every last detail in
this way. Will you believe me when I tell you
that it is all done automatically by computers?
Human beings were not the first to invent computers; Nature has been using them for ages!
The Cosmic computer contains all the essential
data on every creature that exists, and on the basis of his past record it determines when he shall
incarnate and in what country, what kind of
physical body he shall have, what talents and
mental capacities he shall be given and so on.
Then other spirits are assigned to supervise the
proper execution of these decisions. They make
sure that everything takes place exactly as and
when it was planned. If there is to be an 'accident' they wait for the precise moment and, unfailingly, the accident occurs as planned. People
think these things happen by chance, they don't
realize that they have all been planned and cal-
culated in advance with mathematical precision.
If a particular child is to be born in a particular
period, the electronic calculator computes the
astrological data and draws up his birth chart,
and the child is born – and even conceived – according to plan. All the elements in a person's

horoscope correspond exactly to the life he has led and the deeds he has done in previous incarnations: it is this that determines whether he shall know happiness or sorrow, whether he shall be injured in an accident or not, and so on – and it is all determined automatically.

'But then what about liberty?' you may ask. Liberty abides in the spirit; liberty is at work wherever and whenever the spirit manifests itself, modifying the pre-ordained processes, improving or accelerating them. But broadly speaking life is triggered and set in motion in the same way as a motor vehicle. Like a toy train, it runs along the rails, stopping here and there at stations, and coming to a final halt only when the spring has run down. Man is like that clockwork train: he is wound up just enough to live a certain number of years and, like the train, he encounters certain 'obstacles', tunnels or bridges, at different stages of his journey. And all this is planned in advance; even so-called 'chance' encounters are planned. When, all unsuspecting, you are smitten with love 'like a bolt from the blue' and your whole life is turned upside down... Well, that too was planned long ago, long before you were born in fact! Perhaps when you look at a newborn baby you see no sign of it, but that baby has all the equipment, switches,

circuits and 'chips' it needs to carry out its pro-
gramme. A baby is a veritable factory, a State, a
constellation – a whole universe!

It need not surprise you to hear me say that
for one tiny flower to grow and blossom the
whole universe has to give unanimous consent
and provide it with the elements it needs, otherwise it will die. And this is true for you, too. If
you are given favourable spiritual, mental, and
material conditions in which to live, you are
able to grow and flourish, whereas with other
conditions you would be hindered and unable to
develop. Sometimes conditions that are favourable to others are detrimental to you, or conditions detrimental to others are wonderful for
you; you may be gifted with all kinds of qualities and intellectual faculties, but be lacking in
something else, health for instance, all because
some of the forces and currents in the universe
were not in accord with your coming into existence, and they make trouble.

That is why you must work to develop harmony in your lives, you must try to be as harmonious as the stars and every other natural
phenomenon in the universe, otherwise someone or something will forever be causing you
trouble. You may have a perfectly harmonious
relationship with the members of your family
and all your neighbours, but perhaps there are

other people, farther from you, who wish you ill. Perhaps, it is they who are the cause of certain difficulties in your life. Good, you see, is often mixed with evil. And this is why I insist so strongly on the necessity of being in tune with the whole cosmos: so that everything within you may be ideal, so that you may be filled with beauty and light.

Let me give you another example: suppose that, on the one hand, you have a dear friend who loves you and is a true help to you and, on the other hand, an enemy whose one idea is to do your harm. Unfortunately you can never enjoy the one without the other being there: with your friend – or sweetheart – you share some of the best moments of your life, but your enemy brings you only problems, quarrels and distress. So, whether you like it or not, you can't ignore that person, he is part of your life and his influence is detrimental to you. This is why it is important to be in harmony with the whole universe.

Naturally, this is difficult but you can, at least, try! Try, above all, to be in tune with those who are on a higher level, those who guide and order our lives and, secondly, try to achieve harmonious relations with other human beings. This is why the Scriptures tell us: 'Do not let the sun go down on your wrath... before the sun sets, go and forgive your brother.' 'Before the sun sets' means 'before the end of this incarnation', because in later incarnations it is even more difficult to make reparation. It is now, in this life, that we must seek out our enemy and settle our dispute, pay what we owe and then live in peace. Our evil thoughts, feelings and actions are living entities. It is no good pretending they don't exist; they do exist, and they obey our wishes and travel through space until they reach their targets and do their evil work. And then, one day, it is you who have to pay for the harm they have done.

Now let us look for a moment at this idea of our destiny being determined ahead of time. As I have already said in one of my other lectures, we have the opportunity before we come down to earth of changing certain things, providing the Heavenly Hierarchies allow us to, but once we are born, we no longer have that possibility, our lives must unfold as planned, and our entire organism, our nervous, muscular, circulatory systems, our bone structure, our health and our intelligence, all are part of our fixed destiny. If we are born ugly or deformed, we will not have as much in the way of joy, happiness, or success as, for instance, a girl who is born beautiful, gifted, and full of charm. Her destiny will be quite different, she will win the title of 'Miss World', she will be guest of honour at countless receptions, she will be besieged by photographers wherever she goes and, to make her dreams come true, a young and handsome multimillionaire will beg her to marry him!

This is why I say that you cannot change your destiny in this incarnation, but if you start to work now on the next one, if you hope and ask and pray for the next one to be different, it will be. During this incarnation you are limited, but in the next one, you will have everything you long for. It is important that you know this, otherwise you will never do anything to ensure that your next incarnation is an improvement on this one. Why do you suppose that so many people are in such terrible situations? It is because they didn't know how to work in their previous lives, what to work toward, what virtues to develop, what opportunities to ask for in the next life. They were ignorant in their past lives, and if they go on being ignorant in this one, the next incarnation will only be another failure.

Listen carefully to what I say, my dear brothers and sisters; listen and use it for your own good. Make up your minds to profit from the years of life ahead of you. Meditate, hope and pray for all that is best, because in this way you will be launching plans and ideas which will crystallize and take concrete shape in the future. Your present circumstances are the crystallization of other hopes and wishes in the past and they resist change for the time being. This is normal: they cannot be exchanged for new forms until they have served their time and are worn out. But when a man dies, the things he has created in his mind become concrete, they crystallize on the physical plane, and he comes back to earth with all the beauty, intelligence, health and goodness he thought about. His desires materialize in a new form which is as resistant to change as the old one, and resistant also to all destructive and negative forces. What we achieve in our present incarnation is not for now; it is for the future. This is why some of you give way to discouragement. They come and complain to me, saying, 'Master, I have been trying for years now to improve, and nothing ever seems to change. I'm no better than I ever was!' But I tell them, 'You don't understand. In reality you have already changed certain things, but you have to wait for your present form to disappear before the new form can appear. When it does, you will see the fruit of all your hard work and you will be astounded by the beauty and the splendour of what you have achieved!'

Earlier I told you that freedom belongs to the spirit, and now I want to add something to that. Observe the behaviour of an animal or a very young child. An animal obeys the natural laws; it doesn't try to oppose or change the course of events because it has not been given the freedom to do so. An animal, therefore, is obedient, it submits to the laws that govern its species and for that reason it is innocent and blameless. Even when an animal attacks and devours its prey no blame attaches to it; it is acting in accordance with its own nature, it is obeying the laws of Nature. In the same way, a small child, like a baby animal, is still subject to its instincts and impulses; the mind and the will are not yet at work. Only later, when he is older, does a child become capable of choosing either to obey the laws of Nature or to oppose them, either to live in harmony with the Law or to break it.

Now when a man spends all his time eating, sleeping, amusing himself and procreating children; when he works only in order to earn his living then, whatever illusions he may have on the subject, his life is that of an animal: he is governed by instinct and his biological urges. Plants and animals do as much! His life follows its course as though he himself, his consciousness and his will, had no part in it. He goes from

childhood to manhood and from manhood to
old-age, sickness and death without intervening
in any way!

But when a man begins to use his mind consciously and takes command of his instincts,
when he begins to purify and add the spiritual
element to that level of his being, then he becomes a powerful factor, capable of changing his
destiny. But what is destiny? Destiny is an implacable chain of cause and effect to which the
animal, biological, instinctive level of life is subject. What, for instance, is the destiny of a chick-
en? Can a chicken become a king, poet or musi-
cian? No, a chicken is destined for the pot!
Every creature has its own destiny: a wolf is destined to be hunted, trapped and killed or carted
off to the zoo; an ox is destined to be yoked to
the plough, poor beast, and to spend its life toil-
ing in the fields – unless it gets sent to the
slaughterhouse and ends up on someone's plate!
An ox has no hope of changing its destiny any
more than any other animal. Even lambs and
doves have a destiny in keeping with what they
stand for, consistent with their activity and the
elements of which they are formed.

If you want to escape blind subservience to
destiny you must overcome your weakness and
not allow yourself to be enslaved by the lowest
levels of life over which you have no control:

breathing, procreating, eating, drinking and sleeping. This kind of life is very far from the divine. True, it is divine in that it comes from God, for everything comes from God; but in the spiritual sense of the term it is far from divine. Divine life begins at the point where man realizes that he is more than a stomach, a sex organ, a creature of flesh, bone and muscle. Divine life begins when a man realizes that he is also a spiritual being and that he is meant to act and create in the realm of the spirit, that he is meant to devote his life to something more than his physical needs, something sublime, luminous and divine; then, yes, he frees himself from destiny. The destiny of the physical body is to fall ill, die and be left to rot in the grave; on this level there is no escape from destiny. But once a man ceases to be confined to that level, once he ceases to identify himself with his own physical body, he ceases to be bound to destiny.

The spiritual life enables us to add something to our instinctive life and live on a higher plane, a plane beyond the reach of destiny. But to achieve this the spirit must be given the freedom to manifest itself and put its seal and signature on our lives; it must be allowed to have a determining influence on everything we do. In this way we escape the grip of destiny and move onto the level of Providence. Men's bodies are des-

tined to return to dust. Their bodies, yes. But
not their spirits. The spirit is beyond the reach
of destiny, it is governed by the laws of Providence.

The question then arises : what do we have to
do to enter the realm of Providence? First of all
we have to realize that between these two levels,
between destiny and Providence, lies a zone in
which free will must come into play, and that
the principal task of a disciple is to free his will
so completely that it is able to move, work and
be active in the world of the spirit. In this way
the disciple becomes subject to Providence and
finds himself in a position to choose from a vast
array of possibilities, and whatever his choice, it
will always be excellent. Whereas in the realm of
destiny no choice is possible, one is obliged to go
only the one way, the way that leads to destruction, disintegration and annihilation.

All those who are deprived of the light of Initiatic Science continue to flounder in the grip of
destiny. They are continually jostled, oppressed
and tormented : destiny is implacable. Any man,
be he king or emperor, who is subject to destiny,
has to accept its inexorable conclusion – and
heads roll under the guillotine! It is extremely
difficult to escape destiny, for most people have
accumulated a heavy burden of Karmic debts in
their past incarnations and the laws of cause and

effect are absolute. Destiny is blind and without pity, as infallible as a law of physics : if you throw a wine-glass on the floor you know it will be shattered, and the laws of destiny are just as inevitable, just as infallible.

We have every opportunity in this incarnation to create good conditions for the next one, providing we know what to do and do it consciously ; if we do not work in that direction in this incarnation, the next one may be worse than this one. The Church, when it took away the promise of reincarnation, took away the chance for people to improve themselves. Christians have no idea of their potential. They are told that when they die they will go to Heaven (provided they went to Mass regularly) and be seated at the right hand of God – as though it were so easy to win a seat at the right hand of the Almighty! On the other hand, if they neglected their religious duties, they are fated to burn in Hell for all eternity! Why does the Church mislead people like this? Is it to comfort them? It would be far more to the point to tell them the truth!

To summarize : all creatures (and there are many) who let themselves be dominated by their instincts and their physiological needs, who do no spiritual work, will never be able to change their destiny, their lives will unfold as decreed.

Those who work ardently and do all they can to enter the world of love and light may escape. Destiny is cruel and relentless, that is true, but they can rise beyond its reach to subtler regions from which they receive beneficial elements that counteract and neutralize the negative influence of destiny. Of course, you could say that it is still destiny, for Providence is a kind of destiny – but another kind. Providence determines our lives also, but it determines them divinely!

There! All this is extremely important. You now know that if you are content to live like everybody else and never do anything on the higher levels of existence you will not have much hope of changing anything in your destiny since you will be accepting the *status quo*. Perhaps you feel that your destiny is good; that can happen. The destiny of the rich, for instance may seem very good: they live in peace and plenty, no one bothers them, they eat, drink, travel, marry and beget children – what more could anyone ask for? It's the good life! But an Initiate would not agree with that judgment; he knows that that is not the best kind of life. He sees other men labouring, struggling, suffering, stumbling up against innumerable obstacles and bereft of every comfort, and he knows that, in reality, their lives are more worthwhile than the lives of those who live in the lap of luxury.

Human beings have a notion of happiness which is too materialistic, and they are encouraged in this by astrologers who have also been contaminated by materialism. They read your chart, exclaiming, 'Oh, this is wonderful! You have Jupiter in the second house, the Sun in the tenth house, Venus in the seventh. This means that you'll be rich and important, famous and lucky in love: you'll have everything your heart desires!' If they see Squares and Oppositions in your horoscope they predict all kinds of disasters and feel sorry for you – simply because they haven't understood the first thing about it. An Initiate would never give such an interpretation: he would study your chart to see if you were ready to work on the spiritual level, if you were capable of doing God's will and carrying out His divine plan. He doesn't bother about Squares and Oppositions, Detriment or Fall, because it is unimportant.

But most astrologers today are not capable of seeing and interpreting things with the eyes of an Initiate. Like all materialists they are prisoners of the popular conceptions and scale of values: your life is good if you are rich and successful. But material wealth and success are only temporary; none of it lasts long and what happens when it is gone? No, the true merit of a birth-chart is not discernible to all. Some may exclaim

in admiration at a chart which I would find mediocre, because I can see that the person concerned will never do anything worthwhile for the
Kingdom of God: never! Their horoscope
seems to be excellent, promising them talent,
wealth and a prominent social position, but yet
Heaven sees that they are the most ordinary and
insignificant of beings. I wouldn't want to be in
their shoes or have a 'good' horoscope like
theirs! The criteria I use in evaluating a horoscope are unknown to ordinary astrologers.

There are a number of other points I could
mention which make it obvious that astrologers
have a false sense of values. Instead of telling
you, for example, that you have a debt to pay on
a certain level and explaining how you can begin
paying it so as to free yourself from it, they will
tell you how to avoid an accident which is supposed to occur on a certain day. But advice of
that sort will not save you: the accident will
happen if it must, perhaps not on the day they
warned you not to go out, but the next day or
the day before! Karma will not be lied to or
cheated out of its due, so it causes the astrologer
to make a mistake in his calculations.

Perhaps you are wondering what good astrology is if it can't help you to improve your destiny. Astrology can help you to improve your
destiny but not by helping you to run away from

it. It would take too long to explain it fully but at least I can give you just one example to illustrate how this can be. Suppose you owe a large sum of money and you are told that if you fail to pay by a certain date, your furniture and all your belongings will be seized and you will be evicted from your home. With no roof over your head you will be out in the cold, at the mercy of the elements and in danger of falling ill. Rather than standing by, waiting helplessly for fate to catch up with you, you decide to prepare for the day of reckoning by working and saving as much as you possibly can, so that when your debt falls due you are able to pay it and avoid being dispossessed. You can apply the same principle to all levels of existence: if you work and 'save' on the spiritual level you can avoid any accident, illness or financial disaster that may otherwise be in store for you.

Today I have given you some truths which are absolute. Make the most of them, now; study them and ascertain for yourselves the truth of what I say. I am not misleading you. Tremendous possibilities are open to you, and with the help of the Teaching you can learn how to prepare yourselves and how to create a truly glorious future for yourselves.

Self-Limitation – 8. Anarchy and Freedom – 9. The Notion of Hierarchy – 10. The Synarchy Within.

212 – LIGHT IS A LIVING SPIRIT

1. Light : Essence of Creation – 2. The Sun's Rays, their Nature and Activity – 3. Gold is Condensed Sunlight – 4. Light Enables us to See and be Seen – 5. Working with Light – 6. The Prism : a Symbol of Man – 7. Purity Clears the Way for Light – 8. Living with the Intensity of Light – 9. The Spiritual Laser.

213 – MAN'S TWO NATURES, HUMAN AND DIVINE

1. Human Nature or Animal Nature ? – 2.The Lower Self is a Reflection – 3. Man's True Identity – 4. Methods of Escape – 5. The Sun Symbolizes the Divine Nature – 6. Put the Personality to Work – 7. Perfection Comes with the Higher Self – 8. The Silent Voice of the Higher Self – 9. Only by Serving the Divine Nature – 10. Address the Higher Self in Others – 11. Man's Return to God, the Victory.

214 – HOPE FOR THE WORLD : SPIRITUAL GALVANOPLASTY

1. What is Spiritual Galvanoplasty? – 2. Reflections of the Two Principles – 3. Marriages Made in Heaven – 4. Love Freely Given – 5. Love on the Lower Plane – 6. Love on the Higher Plane – 7. Love's Goal is Light – 8. The Solar Nature of Sexual Energy – 9. Mankind Transformed – 10. The Original Experiment and the New One – 11. Replenish the Earth! – 12. Woman's place – 13. The Cosmic Child.

215 – THE TRUE MEANING OF CHRIST'S TEACHING

1. 'Our Father Which Art in Heaven' – 2. 'My Father and I Are One' – 3. 'Be Ye Perfect, Even as Your Father Who is in Heaven is Perfect' – 4. 'Seek Ye First the Kingdom of God and His Justice' – 5. 'On Earth as it is in Heaven' – 6. 'He That Eateth My Flesh and Drinketh My Blood Hath Eternal Life' – 7. 'Father, Forgive Them, For They Know Not What They Do' – 8. 'Unto Him that Smiteth Thee on the One Cheek...' – 9. 'Watch and Pray'.

216 – THE LIVING BOOK OF NATURE

1. The Living Book of Nature – 2. Day and Night – 3. Spring Water or Stagnant Water – 4. Marriage, a Universal Symbol – 5. Distilling the Quintessence – 6. The Power of Fire – 7. The Naked Truth –8. Building a House – 9. Red and White – 10. The River of Life – 11. The New Jerusalem – Perfect Man. I – The Gates. II – The Foundations – 12. Learning to Read and Write.

217 – NEW LIGHT ON THE GOSPELS

1. 'Men do not Put New Wine into Old Bottles' – 2. 'Except Ye Become as Little Children' – 3. The Unjust Stewart – 4. 'Lay up for Yourselves Treasures in Heaven' – 5. The Strait Gate – 6. 'Let Him Which is on the Housetop not Come Down...' – 7. The Calming of the Storm – 8. The First Shall Be Last – 9. The Parable of the Five Wise and the Five Foolish Virgins – 10. 'This is Life Eternal, that they Might Know Thee the Only True God'.

218 – THE SYMBOLIC LANGUAGE OF GEOMETRICAL FIGURES

1. Geometrical Symbolism – 2. The Circle – 3. The Triangle – 4. The Pentagram – 5. The Pyramid – 6. The Cross – 7. The Quadrature of the Circle.

219 – MAN'S SUBTLE BODIES AND CENTRES
the Aura, the Solar Plexus, the Chakras...

1. Human Evolution and the Development of the Spiritual Organs – 2. The Aura – 3. The Solar Plexus – 4. The Hara Centre – 5. Kundalini Force – 6. The Chakras: The Chakra System I. – The Chakra System II. Ajna and Sahasrara.

220 – THE ZODIAC, KEY TO MAN AND TO THE UNIVERSE

1. The Enclosure of the Zodiac – 2. The Zodiac and the Forming of Man – 3. The Planetary Cycle of Hours and Days – 4. The Cross of Destiny – 5. The Axes of Aries–Libra and Taurus–Scorpio – 6. The Virgo–Pisces Axis – 7. The Leo–Aquarius Axis – 8. The Fire and Water Triangles – 9. The Philosophers' Stone : the Sun, the Moon and Mercury – 10. The Twelve Tribes of Israel and the Twelve Labours of Hercules in Relation to the Zodiac.

221 – TRUE ALCHEMY OR THE QUEST FOR PERFECTION

1. Spiritual Alchemy – 2. The Human Tree – 3. Character and Tempe- rament – 4. Our Heritage from the Animal Kingdom – 5. Fear – 6. Stereotypes – 7. Grafting – 8. The Use of Energy – 9. Sacrifice, the Transmutation of Matter – 10. Vainglory and Divine Glory –11. Pride and Humility – 12. The Sublimation of Sexual Energy.

222 – MAN'S PSYCHIC LIFE: ELEMENTS AND STRUCTURES

1. Know Thyself – 2. The Synoptic Table – 3. Several Souls and Several Bodies – 4. Heart, Mind, Soul and Spirit – 5. The Apprenticeship of the Will – 6. Body, Soul and Spirit – 7. Outer Knowledge and Inner Knowledge – 8. From Intellect to Intelligence – 9. True Illumination – 10. The Causal Body – 11. Consciousness–12. The Subconscious – 13. The Higher Self.

223 – CREATION: ARTISTIC AND SPIRITUAL

1. Art, Science and Religion – 2. The Divine Sources of Inspiration – 3. The Work of the Imagination – 4. Prose and Poetry – 5. The Human Voice – 6. Choral Singing – 7. How to Listen to Music – 8. The Magic Power of a Gesture – 9. Beauty – 10. Idealization as a Means of Creation – 11. A Living Masterpiece –12. Building the Temple – Postface.

224 – THE POWERS OF THOUGHT

1. The Reality of Spiritual Work – 2. Thinking the Future – 3. Psychic Pollution – 4. Thoughts are Living Beings – 5. How Thought Produces Material Results – 6. Striking a Balance between Matter and Spirit – 7. The Strength of the Spirit – 8. Rules for Spiritual Work – 9. Thoughts as Weapons – 10. The Power of Concentration – 11. Meditation – 12. Creative Prayer – 13. Reaching for the Unattainable.

225 – HARMONY AND HEALTH

1. Life Comes First – 2. The World of Harmony – 3. Harmony and Health – 4. The Spiritual Foundations of Medicine – 5. Respiration and Nutrition – 6. Respiration: I. The Effects of Respiration on Health – II. How to Melt into the Harmony of the Cosmos – 7. Nutrition on the Different Planes – 8. How to Become Tireless – 9. Cultivate an Attitude of Contentment.

226 – THE BOOK OF DIVINE MAGIC

1. The Danger of the Current Revival of Magic – 2. The Magic Circle of the Aura – 3. The Magic Wand – 4. The Magic Word – 5. Talismans – 6. Is Thirteen an Unlucky Number – 7. The Moon –8. Working with Nature Spirits – 9. Flowers and Perfumes – 10. We All Work Magic – 11. The Three Great Laws of Magic – 12. The Hand – 13. The Power of a Glance – 14. The Magical Power of Trust – 15. Love, the Only True Magic – 16. Never Look for Revenge –17. The Exorcism and Consecration of Objects – 18. Protect Your Dwelling Place.

227 – GOLDEN RULES FOR EVERYDAY LIFE

1. Life: our most precious possession – 2. Let your material life be consistent with your spiritual life – 3. Dedicate your life to a sublime goal – 4. Our daily life: a matter that must be transformed by the spirit – 5. Nutrition as Yoga – 6. Respiration – 7. How to recuperate energy – 8. Love makes us tireless – 9. Technical progress frees man for spiritual work – 10. Furnishing your inner dwelling – 11. The outer world is a

231 – THE SEEDS OF HAPPINESS

1. Happiness: A Gift to be Cultivated – 2. Happiness is not Pleasure – 3. Happiness is Found in Work – 4. A Philosophy of Effort –5. Light Makes for Happiness – 6. The Meaning of Life – 7. Peace and Happiness – 8. If You want to be Happy, Be Alive – 9. Rise Above your Circumstances – 10. Develop a Sensitivity to the Divine – 11. The Land of Canaan – 12. The Spirit is Above the Laws of Fate – 13. Look for Happiness on a Higher Level – 14. The Quest for Happiness is a Quest for God – 15. No Happiness for Egoists – 16. Give Without Expecting Anything in Return – 17. Love Without Asking to be Loved in Return – 18. Our Enemies are Good for Us – 19. The Garden of Souls and Spirits – 20. Fusion on the Higher Planes – 21. We are the Artisans of Our Own Future.

232 – THE MYSTERIES OF FIRE AND WATER

1. The Two Principles of Creation, Water and Fire – 2. The Secret of Combustion – 3. Water, the Matrix of Life – 4. Civilization, a Product of Water – 5. The Living Chain of Sun, Earth and Water – 6. A Blacksmith Works with Fire – 7. Water is Born of Mountains – 8. Physical and Spiritual Water – 9. Feeding the Flame – 10. The Essential Role of Fire – 11. The Cycle of Water: Reincarnation –12. The Cycle of Water: Love and Wisdom – 13. A Candle Flame – 14. How to Light and Tend Fire – 15. Water, the Universal Medium – 16. The Magic Mirror – 17. Trees of Light – 18. The Coming of the Holy Spirit – 19. A Treasury of Pictures.

233 – YOUTH: CREATORS OF THE FUTURE

1. Youth, a World in Gestation – 2. The Foundation Stone of Life: Faith in a Creator – 3. A Sense of the Sacred – 4. The Voice of our Higher Nature – 5. Choosing the Right Direction – 6. Knowledge Cannot Give Meaning to Life – 7. Character Counts for More than Knowledge – 8. Learning to Handle Success and Failure – 9. Recognize the Aspirations of Soul and Spirit – 10. The Divine World, Our Own Inner World – 11. Did you Choose Your Own Family? –12. Benefit From the Experience of Older People – 13. Compare Yourself to Those Who Are Greater – 14. The Will Must be Sustained by Love – 15. Never Admit Defeat – 16. Never Give Way to Despair – 17. Artists of the Future – 18. Sexual Freedom – 19. Preserve the Poetry of Your Love – 20. Members of One Universal Family (I) (II).

234 – TRUTH: FRUIT OF WISDOM AND LOVE

1. The Quest for Truth – 2. Truth, the Child of Wisdom and Love – 3. Wisdom and Love; Light and Warmth – 4. The Love of a Disciple;

235 – 'IN SPIRIT AND IN TRUTH'

236 – ANGELS
and other Mysteries of The Tree of Life

237 – COSMIC BALANCE
The Secret of Polarity

Alternation and Antagonism - The Law of Opposites – 8. 'To Work the Miracles of One Thing' - The Figure of Eight and the Cross – 9. The Caduceus of Hermes - The Astral Serpent – 10. *Iona*, Principle of Life - *Horeb*, Principle of Death – 11.The Triad *Kether-Chesed-Geburah* - Sceptre and Orb - Mind and Heart - A Straight Line and a Curved Line – 12. The Law of Exchange – 13. The Key and the Lock – 14.The Work of the Spirit on Matter - The Holy Grail – 15. Union of the Ego with the Physical Body – 16. The Sacrament of the Eucharist – 17.The Androgynes of Myth – 18. Union with the Universal Soul and the Cosmic Spirit.

By the same author
(translated from the French)

Life Lectures on Tape

KC2510An – The Laws of Reincarnation
   (Two audio cassettes)

(available in French only)

K 2001 Fr – La science de l'unité
K 2002 Fr – Le bonheur
K 2003 Fr – La vraie beauté
K 2004 Fr – L'éternel printemps
K 2005 Fr – La loi de l'enregistrement
K 2006 Fr – La science de l'éducation
K 2007 Fr – La prière
K 2008 Fr – L'esprit et la matière
K 2009 Fr – Le monde des archétypes
K 2010 Fr – L'importance de l'ambiance
K 2011 Fr – Le yoga de la nutrition
K 2012 Fr – L'aura
K 2013 Fr – Déterminisme et indéterminisme
K 2014 Fr – Les deux natures de l'être humain
K 2015 Fr – Prendre et donner
K 2016 Fr – La véritable vie spirituelle
K 2017 Fr – La mission de l'art
K 2018 Fr – Il faut laisser l'amour véritable se manifester
K 2019 Fr – Comment orienter la Frorce sexuelle
K 2020 Fr – Un haut idéal pour la jeunesse
K 2021 Fr – La réincarnation – Preuves de la réincarnation
   dans les Evangiles
K 2022 Fr – La réincarnation – Rien ne se produit par hasard,
   une intelligence préside à tout
K 2023 Fr – La réincarnation – L'aura et la réincarnation
K 2024 Fr – La loi de la responsabilité
K 2551 Fr – La réincarnation   (coffret 3 cassettes)
K 2552 Fr – Introduction à l'astrologie initiatique
K 2553 Fr – La méditation   (coffret 3 cassettes)

Editor-Distributor

Editions PROSVETA S.A. - B.P. 12 - 83601 Fréjus Cedex (France)

Tel. 04 94 40 82 41 - Télécopie 04 94 40 80 05 - E-Mail: international@prosveta.com

Distributors

AUSTRALIA
QUEST, 484 Kent Street
2000 Sydney

AUSTRIA
HARMONIEQUELL VERSAND
A- 5302 Henndorf Hof 37
Tel and fax (43) 6214 7413

BELGIUM
PROSVETA BENELUX
Liersesteenweg 154 B-2547 Lint
Tel (32) 3/455 41 75 Fax 3/454 24 25
N.V. MAKLU Somersstraat 13-15
B-2000 Antwerpen
Tel. (32) 34 55 41 75
VANDER S.A.
Av. des Volontaires 321
B-1150 Bruxelles
Tel. (32) 27 62 98 04 Fax 27 62 06 62

BRAZIL
NOBEL SA – Rua da Balsa, 559
CEP 02910 - São Paulo, SP

BULGARIA
SVETOGLED
Bd Saborny 16 A appt 11 – 9000 Varna

CANADA
PROSVETA Inc. – 3950, Albert Mines
North Hatley (Qc), J0B 2C0
Tel. (819) 564-3287 Fax. (819) 564-1823
in Canada, call toll free: 1-800-584-8212
E-Mail: prosveta@colba.net

COLUMBIA
PROSVETA
Avenida 46 n° 19 - 14 (Palermo)
Santafe de Bogotá
Tel. (57) 232-01-36 – Fax (57) 633-58-03

CYPRUS
THE SOLAR CIVILISATION BOOKSHOP
73 D Kallipoleos Avenue - Lycavitos
P. O. Box 4947, 1355 – Nicosia
Tel: 02 377503 and 09 680854

GERMANY
PROSVETA Deutschland
Postfach 16 52 – 78616 Rottweil
Tel. 0741-46551 – Fax. 0741-46552
eMail: Prosveta.de@t-online.de
EDIS GmbH, Daimlerstr 5
82054 Sauerlach
Tel. (49) 8104-6677-0
Fax. (49) 8104-6677-99

GREAT BRITAIN
PROSVETA
The Doves Nest, Duddleswell Uckfield,
East Sussex TN 22 3JJ
Tel. (01825) 712988 - Fax (01825) 713386
E-Mail: prosveta@pavilion.co.uk

GREECE
EDITIONS PROSVETA – J. VAMVACAS
El. Venizelou 4 – 18531 - Athens

HOLLAND
STICHTING PROSVETA NEDERLAND
Zeestraat 50
2042 LC Zandvoort

HONG KONG
SWINDON BOOK CO LTD.
246 Deck 2, Ocean Terminal
Harbour City – Tsimshatsui, Kowloon

IRELAND
PROSVETA
The Doves Nest
Duddleswell Uckfield,
East Sussex TN 22 3JJ, U.K.

ITALY
PROSVETA Coop.
Casella Postale
06060 Moiano (PG)

LUXEMBOURG
PROSVETA BENELUX
Liersesteenweg 154 B-2547 Lint

NORWAY
PROSVETA NORDEN
Postboks 5101 – 1501 Moss

NEW ZEALAND
PSYCHIC BOOKS
p.o. Box 87-151
Meadowbank, Auckland 5

PORTUGAL
PUBLICAÇÕES
EUROPA-AMERICA Ltd
Est Lisboa-Sintra KM 14
2726 Mem Martins Codex

ROMANIA
ANTAR
Str. N. Constantinescu 10
Bloc 16A - sc A - Apt. 9
Sector 1 - 71253 Bucarest

SPAIN
ASOCIACIÓN PROSVETA ESPAÑOLA
C/ Ausias March n° 23 Ático
SP-08010 Barcelona
Tel (34) (3) 412 31 85 - Fax (3) 302 13 72

SWITZERLAND
PROSVETA
Société Coopérative
CH - 1808 Les Monts-de-Corsier
Tel. (41) 21 921 92 18
Fax. (41) 21 922 92 04
e-Mail: prosveta@swissonline.ch

UNITED STATES
PROSVETA USA, Inc.—P.O. Box 1176
New Smyrna Beach, FL 32170-1176
Web : www.prosveta-usa.com
E-mail : sales@prosveta-usa.com

VENEZUELA
Betty Munöz Urbanización Los Corales - avenida Principal
Quinta La Guarapa - LA GUAIRA - Municipio Vargas

PRINTED IN FRANCE IN JUNE 1998
EDITIONS PROSVETA, Z.I. DU CAPITOU
B.P.12 – 83601 FRÉJUS
FRANCE

– N° d'impression: 2478 –
Dépôt légal: Juin 1998
Printed in France